Survival & Liberation

Survival & Liberation

Pastoral Theology in African American Context

Carroll A. Watkins Ali

Chalice Press

St. Louis, Missouri

Biblical quotations, unless otherwise noted, are from the *New Revised Standard Version Bible*, copyright 1989, Division of Christian Education of the National Council of Churches of Christ in the USA. Used by permission.

Scripture quotations marked (NIV) are taken from the Holy Bible, New International Version® NIV®. Copyright© 1973, 1978, 1984 by International Bible Society. Used by permission of Zondervan Publishing House. All rights reserved.

Cover design: Elaine Young
Cover art: Robert Anthony Ketchens
Interior design: Rhonda Dohack
Art direction: Michael Domínguez

10 9 8 7 6 5 4 3 2 1   99 00 01 02 03

This book is printed on acid-free, recycled paper.

Visit Chalice Press on the World Wide Web at
www.chalicepress.com

Library of Congress Cataloging–in–Publication Data

Watkins Ali, Carroll A.
    Survival and Liberation : Pastoral Theology in African American Context / by Carroll A. Watkins Ali.
        p.   cm.
    ISBN 0-8272-3443-0
    1. Pastoral theology 2. Afro-Americans—Religion.   I. Title.
    BV4011.A45   1999   99–30856
                                                              C1P

Printed in the United States of America

To my parents,
Izear and Rose Watkins,
and to
Mother Addie Thomas

Contents

Acknowledgments

I wish to express my heartfelt appreciation and gratitude to Jane I. Smith, who as academic dean of Iliff School of Theology encouraged me to consider the doctoral work out of which this work was birthed. I am also grateful for the guidance of my advisor, Larry Kent Graham, throughout the doctoral program and the process of finishing my dissertation. From the very beginning, it was clear that Dr. Graham believed in the importance of my work. Of course, there would be no accomplishment without the financial assistance of the Fund for Theological Education (FTE). I will eternally be grateful to the former director of FTE, Oscar McCloud, for his leadership of the fund, and to those African American scholars who not only supported FTE financially, but also with their time and talents as mentors to upcoming religious scholars.

A special thanks is due to all of the supporting cast of scholars in my life, beginning with the other members of my committee. Jacquelyn Grant, Arthur C. Jones, and Joretta Marshall read and gave helpful feedback on the manuscript as it evolved through many stages. Words cannot adequately express my gratitude to Dr. Grant for taking time away from a demanding schedule to graciously extend womanist care that informed and undergirded my efforts to appropriate womanist thought to the field of pastoral theology. Dr. Jones was also very busy with very important projects, yet never too busy to thoughtfully respond from a psychological perspective. His way of being present with the text helped me to listen for the wisdom of the ancestors. Joretta Marshall faithfully asked important questions challenging me to be prepared with adequate answers as the pastoral theological dialogue entertained a new perspective. Others without whose encouragement and scholarly assistance (even though many are from other academic disciplines) I could not have made it to this point are: Rufus Burrow, Jr., Lee Butler, Jr., Christine Chao, Jean Dalby Clift, Wallace Clift, James H. Cone, Sandra Dixon, H. Edward Everding, Jr., Marsha Foster Boyd, Will Gravely, Vincent Harding, Cindy Lynch, Clarice Martin, Aminah McCloud, Bonnie Miller-McLemore, Jean Miller Schmidt, Archie Smith, Jr., John Spangler, Bernie Spilka, Cheryl Townsend Gilkes, Theodore D. Walker, Jr., and the late James Washington. To each of these persons I owe a debt of my deepest gratitude.

Jon Berquist at Chalice Press has been supportive in ways only an editor can be. I appreciate his willingness to work with a new author and his encouragement throughout the process of bringing this book to production. Most of all, his sensitivity to the subject matter is quite gratifying to me.

I cannot fail to acknowledge a host of caregivers and extended family who encouraged and supported me and my children in their own special ways: Rev. Deborah Thompson, Elder Patrick Demmer, Sr., Glynis Hawkins, Milt and Jennie McCrone, Faith Royal, Elder Emmitt and Mrs. Ruth Searuggs, James Clark, Daniel Muse, Kiboko Kiboko, Angela Webb, James Charleston, Barbara Hughes, Deborah Johnston, Cheryl Butler, James Caldwell, Rev. Sandra Daniel, Elder Marvin and Mrs. Nettie Fisher, Rev. Charles Webb, Rev. Reginald and Mrs. Betsy Holmes, Linda Smallwood, Roland and Carol Jean Baptiste, Pamela Love, Elizabeth Lockman, Reginald and Leslie Chapman, and those "prayer warriors" of Park Hill Christian Church and members of the "Choices, Challenges, and Images" family over the years. Last, yet first in so many respects of modeling what it means to give and love unconditionally, Mother Addie Thomas (my adopted spiritual mother and church mother to so many) represents the best of the womanist tradition in my life. I have so many happy memories of times spent in her nurturing presence; and even now as she barely recognizes me in her advanced years she continues to offer me hope and encouragement.

Finally, I acknowledge that I am blessed to have been born into such an endearing family. At an early age, my loving and committed parents, Izear and Rose Watkins, instilled in me a belief in myself. They were also very intentional about making me consciously aware of the realities of life that I would be confronted with as a female African American, teaching me a respect for those who came before me and giving me a concern for the survival and liberation of African Americans. My sisters Sheila, Pamela (Nubia), Grace, and Lynda, helped to reinforce those values as sibling rivals and through their examples of strong Black womanhood in relation to our parents, their spouses, their children, and my children. These four women have always cheered me on toward my best efforts at living this life.

My children Kenny (Ward), Teisha, and Kali have been my inspiration and motivation ever since I first looked into each of their eyes. They have also been my most ardent supporters (often making great sacrifices) and the keepers of my dreams.

My husband, Abdur-Rahim Ali, and stepchildren Kareem, Malik, Hanniyah, Abdur-Rahim Ibn, and Leenah came into my life at a point when academic work and writing almost consumed me. I know that there were times that were trying, but I am grateful that they, too, managed to hang in there with me in spite of my shortcomings.

Preface

The impetus for this book emerges out of my own awareness as an African American woman that, as we approach the end of the twentieth century, the masses of Black people in the United States of America live in a crisis state. In the initial stages of my thinking about pastoral theology in the African American context, it was quite obvious to me that current paradigms of pastoral theology and care—in their individualistic approaches—are inadequate for the pastoral care needs of African Americans collectively. Mindful of the critical existential dilemma facing the masses of African Americans today, the logical questions for pastoral theological reflection are: What should characterize pastoral theology in the African American context? and What are the essential guidelines for African American pastoral care?

Eventually, other questions came to mind: Who determines what pastoral theology is? and Whose pastoral theology is it? The more I considered these questions, the clearer the importance of context became. I began to understand why traditional models for pastoral theology and care are inadequate for the crises of Black life in America. Basically, traditional paradigms of pastoral theology and care were informed almost exclusively by European American cultural thought, which has been dominant in American society. Many of the cultural particularities of the African American context have not been considered, especially the fact that it is a culture that has been oppressed.

Therefore, the premise of this book is that pastoral theology is different from context to context. A guiding assumption is that it is the *experience* within a cultural context that determines which sources are appropriate for the development of pastoral theology in that context. This book, then, is intended to broaden the pastoral theological discussion. It asserts that the very real *survival and liberation* issues of contemporary African Americans are a task for pastoral theological reflection. Throughout the book much of my discussion raises issues and concerns in direct reponse to theories developed by Seward Hiltner that ultimately became the basis for much of traditional pastoral theological method. My primary objective is to introduce the significance of womanist thought for pastoral theology as it brings the experience of African Americans, through the eyes of poor Black women, to the forefront of pastoral theological dialogue.

CHAPTER 1

Introduction

We have to keep in mind at all times that we are not fighting for integration, nor are we fighting for separation. We are fighting for recognition as human beings. We are fighting for the right to live as free humans in this society.

El-Hajj Malik Shabazz (Malcolm X)

Descendants of African people, who arrived on the shores of North America as import for slave trade, have sustained a struggle for *survival and liberation* in this sector of the world for nearly four hundred years.[1] This book is an inquiry into the African American experience for the purpose of building a conceptual framework for pastoral theology in the African American context that is adequate to the struggle of many African Americans to stay alive and be free of the oppression of racial injustice.

Given the often critical nature of existence within the African American context, the concepts of *survival* and *liberation* together point to the need for pastoral theological reflection on

---

[1] I am concentrating on people of African descent who reside in the United States of America. The terms *African, African American,* and *Black* will be used interchangeably throughout this book in reference to this population. The intent is to focus on the racial experience of Black people in this country as a whole.

1

the indigenous experience of the African American context. For the purposes of this text, what is meant by the term *survival* is the ability of African Americans (1) to resist systematic oppression and genocide and (2) to recover the self, which entails a psychological recovery from the abuse and dehumanization of political oppression and exploitation as well as recovery of African heritage, culture, and values that were repressed during slavery. By *liberation*, I mean (1) total freedom from all kinds of oppression for African descendants of slaves and (2) the ability of African Americans as a people to self-determine and engage in the process of transformation of the dominant oppressive culture through political resistance.[2]

Resources for pastoral theology that promote the *survival and liberation* of African Americans must be attuned to the African American experience and, therefore, must emerge primarily from sources indigenous to the African American context. In this book, I will develop a conceptual framework for a new paradigm in pastoral theological method that will take seriously the specifics of the African American context.

The Womanist Perspective

Traditional models of pastoral theology have not factored in the oppression of racism, sexism, and classism that poor African American women have to contend with in their daily lives. Although the liberation perspective, which primarily represents an African American male point of view, can be accounted for in pastoral theological literature to some

---

[2] In the formulation of my thoughts about what is meant by *survival and liberation*, I have been influenced by Black liberation perspectives and womanist perspectives in general. However, I have been deeply influenced by bell hooks's use of the term *self-recovery*. See bell hooks, *Sisters of the Yam* (Boston: South End Press, 1993). Vincent Harding's ideas on social transformation (as taught in courses at the Iliff School of Theology) have also stimulated my thinking. Some of these ideas show up in his book *Hope and History*. See Vincent Harding, *Hope and History* (Maryknoll, N.Y.: Orbis Books, 1990). Finally, some explanation is required as to why I speak of *survival and liberation* in political terms as I write about pastoral theology: In view of the critical social, economic, and political dilemma of African Americans, pastoral theological method must be immediate and prophetic in praxis. At the core of the Black struggle is a call for political transformation of American society.

extent,[3] as well as the feminist perspective of White women, the unique perspective that has been formed by the experience of Black women from slavery to the present time is absent from the dialogue.

It is the voice of the poor Black woman in America that says that the *survival and liberation* of African Americans is an urgent pastoral theological concern at this point in time. The perspective of African American women who are poor—a voice among other marginal voices of American society—has not been heard in the academic dialogue of pastoral theology.[4]

By way of introducing the womanist perspective, which incorporates the perspective of poor Black women in America, my aim is to resist the individualistic trap of traditional pastoral theological method, which usually presents individual case material upon which to reflect. However, I think that it is appropriate to share meaningful narrative from one Black woman's story in order to begin the dialogue.

Nonetheless, I do so by cautioning the reader not to think in terms of this particular woman's story in an individualistic way. That is to say, her story should not be treated as an isolated incident. Rather, it is representative of the stories of a disproportionate number of African American women who share a common existential dilemma because they are Black, female, and economically oppressed. Therefore, this woman's story is multiplied many times over in the African American context. The main point that should be remembered is the reality that this woman's critical life issues are, as the issues of far too many poor African American women are, left unaddressed by current paradigms of pastoral theology and care. Following is a

---

[3] Liberation from oppression has been presented as criterion for pastoral theology by other African American authors. See James H. Harris, *Pastoral Theology: A Black Church Perspective* (Minneapolis: Fortress Press, 1991); Archie Smith, Jr., *The Relational Self: Ethics and Therapy From a Black Perspective* (Nashville: Abingdon Press, 1982); Gayraud Wilmore, "Black Theology and Pastoral Ministry," *The Pastor As Theologian*, eds. Earl E. Shelp and Ronald S. Sunderland (New York: Pilgrim Press, 1988); Edward Wimberly and Anne Streaty Wimberly, *Liberation And Human Wholeness: The Conversion Experience of Black in Slavery and Freedom* (Nashville: Abingdon Press, 1986).

[4] See Bonnie J. Miller-McLemore, "The Human Web: Reflections on the State of Pastoral Theology," *The Christian Century*, April 7, 1993.

portion of an African American woman's narrative whom I will call Lemonine. Lemonine spent three years in therapy with me prior to her untimely death.[5]

One Who Had So Much to Give and Live...

Lemonine was in her early forties when she died. She left behind two children, a daughter in her early twenties and a son in his last year of high school. She had raised both of them as a single parent most of their lives. She also left a toddler grand-daughter whom she was resigned to raise if she had to, aging parents (who divorced when she was a child), and a sister from whom she felt estranged.

For all appearances, Lemonine was a middle-class Black woman. She was well educated, articulate, and very talented—an artist. She was quite attractive in personality and in the way she put herself together—impeccably groomed, stylish. However, the truth of the matter was that Lemonine was a poor Black woman—economically oppressed by her life circumstances. She lived with the reality that missing one paycheck from her corporate position would put her and her family on the streets. Her reality was that there was never enough money to make ends meet. She virtually lived in fear of the next time that the

---

[5] I have selected to share narratives from the lives of three African American women in the course of this book. I was given written permission to use this material. These stories are composites of true experience, but are not linked to any identifiable living individual. The names have been changed with the exception of Pauletta, who gave permission for her real name to be used. The portion of their stories that I relate here may not be as complete as some would like. The reader will note that I do not go into the details of how it happens that these women are single mothers. There is a reason for that. I want to dignify their lives. I want the reader to look at their stories and resist the temptation to check off points that may fit into stereotypical views about single Black women. Truly, it matters not who is/was married (and how many times) and who is/was not married. What matters is that these are stories of single African American women with children in this society who are in crisis. Nonetheless, there is a wealth in these stories that, in addition to their pastoral care needs, speaks to their dignity as they struggle with their victimizations. Although I refer to their victimization, I hope the reader can see that they do not see themselves as mere victims, but that they struggle daily with that victimization. It is true that many African Americans have overcome such difficulties, but it is also true that far too many have not. Therefore, I have no problem with using the words *poor* and *victim* to describe their circumstances. I have more of a problem with their realities. It is my hope that putting these women's issues (while in therapy with me) before the reader will serve to enlighten and make relevant points about the pastoral care needs of many African Americans.

already-too-old car would break down or would be stolen again by gang members because they identified with its color. Health was another major concern that Lemonine worried about, and she literally worried herself sick. The year prior to entering therapy she had been hospitalized for extreme physical exhaustion. Often Lemonine wondered aloud, "Where is the money going to come from?"

Lemonine was very quick to acknowledge that her existence was not anywhere near middle class. Yet, she kept up the appearance. She could not afford to pay for therapy, but she was resourceful enough to find someone like me who was willing to work with her regardless. She appeared vibrant (something that she had mastered) and looked the picture of health. Not many would believe (except other poor Black women like herself) that things were as desperate as they were for Lemonine.

Truly, *life* was Lemonine's presenting problem. There are no other diagnoses in the traditional sense. Lemonine was basically suffering from being overcome by her own personal life, while trying to cope with all the external social realities that affected each age group of her family members. In essence, each weekly session during our relationship served mainly to build Lemonine up enough so that she could go back out to face a hostile world for another week. A major issue that came up often in our sessions was the racism Lemonine experienced in her workplace. In fact, she experienced tremendous stress related to the dynamics of both racism and sexism in corporate America. The glass ceiling barred heavily against her advancement before she could even get her foot in the door because she was both Black and female. She worried about being the last hired and the first fired as a result of corporate downsizing. This actually occurred twice during the course of our sessions.

In retrospect, it now seems that therapy was Lemonine's last effort to find a way to overcome the many problems of her world. She had searched for a church body to join but felt that she had not been able to identify a church that met her spiritual needs or that gave her the level of comfort she was seeking (partly because of the lack of affirmation from pastors for what she believed were her own gifts for ministry). I now realize that

I witnessed Lemonine lose hope and give up on life altogether. Eventually, we mutually agreed to terminate therapy. Her medical doctor prescribed an antidepressant, and she joined an informal discussion group on metaphysics that she felt would fill the void. My hope was that Lemonine would continue to practice the cognitive coping skills we had worked on over the three years of her therapy. Six months later, Lemonine was gone! She developed a brain tumor, and it seems she died almost overnight.

I have searched my mind time and again trying to think of what more I could have done or what I could have done differently to help Lemonine. The truth is that I did all I could possibily do within my professional capacity as a pastoral counselor. What I was able to do as an individual was limited. It is very clear to me that a communal strategy of a network of care and resources was required to meet Lemonine's needs.

For those whose response to Lemonine's story may still be that a woman does not have to be African American to have to face these kinds of issues, the point is that more often than not the cultural experience of the majority of African American women contends with issues similiar to Lemonine's. Therefore, Lemonine's life is symptomatic of what is a direct result of the racial oppression experienced by African American people as a whole. That is not to negate or diminish the legacy of achievement of many African Americans despite their oppression,[6] but to acknowledge the disproportionate numbers of Black people in this country who struggle to overcome the odds waged against them. More will be shared about the social location of poor African American women in general in chapter 2.

The Womanist Approach to Pastoral Theology

To speak of communal strategies and approaches in terms of Black women's experience is to present a womanist perspective to the field of pastoral theology. The womanist perspective is derived from a school of thought that has been advancing,

---

[6] For a thorough overview of the accomplishments and achievements of African Americans, see Andrew Billingsley, *Climbing Jacob's Ladder: The Enduring Legacy of African American Families* (New York: Simon & Schuster, 1992).

primarily, in the scholarship of African American women across disciplines. However, its earliest academic development began in the religious scholarship of African American women. Eventually, the nomenclature of *womanist* was adopted from Pulitzer Prize winner Alice Walker's use of it. Walker coined the term and defined what a womanist was in clear distinction from White women's meanings for the term *feminist*. Basically, Walker's definition is designed to encompass the worldview of Black women in this country descendent from Africans brought to this country as slaves.[7]

In addition to the use of stories about strong Black women figures and other historical data that point to a womanist tradition among Black women, womanist scholars have also appropriated portions of Walker's three-part definition of womanist into their writings in their respective disciplines. The specific portion of the definition that most easily lends itself to a womanist appropriation for the field of pastoral theology and care is the following excerpt taken from the second part of Walker's statement of what it means to be womanist:

> Committed to survival and wholeness of entire people, male and female. Not a separatist, except periodically for health. Traditionally universalist, as in: "Mama, why are we brown, pink, and yellow, and our cousins are white, beige, and black?" Ans.: "Well, you know the colored race is just like a flower garden, with every color flower represented." Traditionally capable, as in: "Mama, I am walking to Canada, and I am taking you and a bunch of other slaves with me." Reply: "It wouldn't be the first time."[8]

This excerpt clearly expresses the womanist concern for survival and liberation of African Americans as a race. It implies that racial injustice from a womanist perspective encompasses any kind of oppression that threatens the survival and/or limits the liberty of Black people as a whole. There are even

---

[7] Alice Walker, *In Search of Our Mothers' Gardens: Womanist Prose* (San Diego: Harcourt Brace Jovanovich, 1983), xi–xii.

[8] Ibid., xi.

suggested strategies for the health and overall well-being of African Americans, making them a communal concern.

In light of the above statement of Walker's definition, Lemonine comes back to mind. Her needs were critical life and death issues that were left unaddressed. Is it possible that her outcome could have been quite different had there been a community of insistent caregivers willing to provide her the space and to indentify the resources to make her health issues a first priority? In practical terms Lemonine needed intervention from a support system that would have allowed her to separate herself from the overwhelming external pressures long enough for her to regain her health. She needed resources and people to help take care of her and her family during her recovery period. She needed advocates to make changes wherever possible in the structures of American society to make the quality of her life more equitable and, therefore, endurable.

New Method for Pastoral Theology in the African American Context

Lemonine's story in light of the larger African American community illustrates how an approach that primarily focuses on the duties and activities of the individual clergyperson in relation to the needs of individuals fails in the African American context. What are the implications for pastoral theological method when the reality is that the crisis presents a communal concern rather than an individualistic concern?

Basically, a new method for pastoral theology in the African American context that addresses the communal needs for survival and liberation (1) begins with the experience of the culture versus objectifications and abstractions about the culture, (2) allows for the significance of communality versus individuality, and (3) expands the operations of ministry.

First, the individual pastoral caregiver's experience in the context of ministry (particularly from a dominant culture perspective) is at least one step removed from the actual experience of those inhabiting the context. Therefore, an awareness of the subjective experience of the cultural context is necessary to modify and/or correct the objective experience of the pastoral caregiver.

Second, the communal concern for the majority of African Americans requires a community effort or a network of caregivers working with the pastor/pastoral caregiver. Even when dealing with an individual such as Lemonine it is quite clear that the resources needed are beyond the scope of an individual caregiver. There also needs to be ongoing provisions for persons whose critical needs are extended over a long duration.

Third, the pastoral care needs of the African American context require an expansion of the traditional aspects of shepherding beyond healing, sustaining, and guiding.[9] In essence, the pastoral care of Black Americans, who are faced with critical concerns involved in the struggle for survival and liberation, needs to expand to include functions that are also *nurturing, empowering*, and, ultimately, *liberating* in praxis. The act of *reconciling* may also need to be revisited in the African American context as an act of the first order for ministry between African Americans themselves.[10] More will be said about the *who* and *what* that needs to be reconciled in the African American context along with the need for nurture, empowerment, and liberation in chapter 7, which provides guidelines for pastoral care in the African American context.

---

[9] Lacking another metaphor besides that of *shepherd*, I am still working somewhat within the framework of Seward Hiltner's systematic approach, which is dependent on the metaphor of shepherd. For the time being, I recognize that it can be argued that the new aspects of ministry that will expand beyond Hiltner's healing, sustaining, and guiding can be stretched in meaning to fit in with the acts of a shepherd toward sheep.

[10] Others have already addressed the need to expand the aspects of shepherding or the approach to pastoral care in general; for example, "reconciling" was offered as the fourth function. See William A. Clebsch and Charles R. Jaekles, *Pastoral Care In Historical Perspective* (Englewood Clifts, N.J.: Prentice Hall., 1964), 56–66. Howard Clinebell does not address the aspects of shepherding specifically, but he introduces a "liberation growth model" for pastoral care and counseling that says, "the overarching goal of all pastoral care and counseling (and of all ministry) is to liberate, empower, and nurture wholeness centered in the spirit." See Howard Clinebell, *Basic Types of Pastoral Care and Counseling* (Nashville: Abingdon Press, 1984), 26.

New Definition for Pastoral Theology

A new method implies a new definition for pastoral theology as well. Contemporary definitions for pastoral theology vary depending upon their understanding of the purpose and/or the content for theological reflection that is relevant to pastoral situations. Here are three traditional views of pastoral theology. (1) A theological enterprise in the formulation of "practical principles, theories, and procedures for ordained ministry in all of its functions." That is to say, the purpose of theological reflection is to set forth an accepted process through which ministry in general is administered. (2) "The practical theological discipline concerned with theory and practice of pastoral care and counseling." This approach considers pastoral theology to be an arm of practical theology around which theological reflection is organized for the development of praxis for pastoral caregiving. And (3) "a form of theological reflection in which pastoral experience serves as context for critical development of theological understanding."[11]

Seward Hiltner, who is considered the founding father of pastoral theology as a discipline, defined pastoral theology as "that branch or field of theological knowledge and inquiry that brings the shepherding perspective to bear on all the operations and functions of the church and minister, and then draws conclusions of a theological order from reflection on these observations."[12] Specifically, Hiltner's definition introduces the concept of the "shepherding perspective" as a way of thinking about "pastoral experience."

In order to adequately address the needs of the African American context, a new definition for pastoral theology is defined as theological reflection on the experience of the cultural context as relevant for strategic pastoral caregiving in the context of ministry. Pastoral theology defined this way elevates the importance of contextuality, asserting that the experience of the cultural context is central to theological reflection. Hence, the

---

[11]Rodney J. Hunter, ed., *Dictionary of Pastoral Care and Counseling* (Nashville: Abingdon Press, 1990), 867.

[12]See Seward Hiltner, *Preface to Pastoral Theology: The Ministry and Theory Shepherding* (New York: Abingdon Press, 1958), 20.

definition creates a major shift from Hiltner's definition in that the primary focus is the contextual cultural experience.

Primarily, the new definition asserts that the more appropriate point of departure for theological reflection begins with a focus on the experience indigenous to the cultural context. Second, it suggests that pastoral theological reflection is at least a two-step process that puts the experience of the people inhabiting the context for ministry ahead of the experience of the pastoral caregiver in the ministry context. That is to say, primary consideration is given to theological questions that are brought to bear on the experience of those inhabiting the cultural context of ministry; and the experience of the pastoral caregiver in relation to the needs of the cultural context becomes the secondary object of theological reflection.

The new definition acknowledges that times have indeed changed since Hiltner asserted his definition of pastoral theology. It is instructive to note that Hiltner wrote during the so called *modern era* when dominant cultural views were accepted as normative for the conceptualization of theory. It should also be noted that as time advances toward a new millennium, we need to usher in the *postmodern era*.[13] With the advance of the postmodern era comes an acknowledgment that knowledge is relative to cultural awarenesses. Hence, the question of contextuality is reconsidered and emphasized (in light of contemporary issues such as those in the African American context) as a part of the new approach to method.

---

[13] The issue of modern versus postmodern in academia is still pretty much up in the air as far as definitions, approach, etc., go. However, based on a discussion with Charles Long and Theodore Walker (during an American Academy of Religion meeting several years ago) on this subject, I am convinced that the field of pastoral theology is in transition from the modern era into the postmodern era as far as scholarship goes. It is significant that at the time of Hiltner's writing, problems of race-gender-class oppressions were not addressed. That is, during Hiltner's time (which I am calling the modern era) scholarship was done from a dominant cultural perspective without these kinds of considerations. Now that the field of pastoral theology is beginning to consider race-gender-class issues, there appears to be a growing awareness that knowledge is relative across cultures. To the extent that this is acknowledged and incorporated into scholarship, the more the field will transit into the postmodern era—an era in which race-gender-class does not present problems for conceptual theory.

The Question of a Master/Umbrella Perspective

The recognition that there needs to be a paradigm for pastoral theology that places the issues of contextuality before perspectival considerations raises a question once visited by Hiltner of whether or not the concept of a "master perspective" is appropriate. Hiltner's method avoids the idea of a master perspective that would subsume the perspectives of shepherding, communicating, and organizing ministry under one umbrella perspective. His argument was that the concept of a master perspective is too complicated and, ultimately, diminishing of each of the other perspectives. Therefore, Hiltner's choice, which has become the traditional approach, is to make the sheperding perspective (pastors' perspective) the dominant perspective for ministry.[14]

On the contrary, this book asserts that the concept of a master perspective is useful to the enterprise of African American pastoral theology. It implies that each perspective of ministry should be cognizant of and sensitive to the cultural particularities of the ministry context. Along the same lines it is instructive to note that for the African American context the word "master" has negative connotations held over from the memory of the slavery experience. Therefore, it is more culturally sensitive to speak in terms of an umbrella perspective instead of a master perspective to identify the primary cultural perspective of a given cultural context. That is, the purpose of an umbrella perspective is to ensure that an awareness of the subjective experience of those living in the cultural context of ministry guides the events of ministry.

For the purposes of this book, the umbrella perspective of African American culture that is presented as the guiding factor, especially for the pastoral care needs of the majority of Blacks, *is the perspective of poor Black women.* Inasmuch as poor Black women (and their children) are positioned at the lowest levels of social, political, and economic status in this country, it is their eyes through which pastoral caregivers need to gain a view of what the critical needs are in Black America. It is essential

---

[14] Hiltner, 61.

that the perspective of poor Black women overshadow the paternalism left over from the modern era, which holds to the tradition that the pastor's experience offers the best view of the ministry context for theological reflection. And it is essential that the perspective of poor Black women outweigh the dominant European American cultural thought, which puts the concerns of the individual ahead of the concerns of the whole of communality and overlooks the racism, sexism, and classism that is prevalent in American society. Finally, it is also the perspective of poor Black women that must also inform the character of ministry in the African American context.

Implicitly, the umbrella perspective arises from the experience of poor Black women in America, which is the most appropriate point of departure for pastoral theological reflection in the African American context. As we consider the cultural specifics of the experience of poor Black women, therein lies the significance for the change in methodology that calls for a communal approach to ministry (both in terms of those who give pastoral care and those who receive it). Therein lies the mandate that every act of ministry in the African American context should concern itself with the *survival and liberation* needs of all Black people in this country. And therein comes the call for an approach to ministry in which the content of ministry is expanded beyond the traditional aspects of shepherding in order to meet the critical needs of the African American context.

Correlating Cognate Sources

Consistent with the new paradigm's emphasis on contextuality, this book proposes a methodology for African American pastoral theology that incorporates the use of secondary cognate resources that are indigenous to the African American context. Inasmuch as there is such a tremendous void in the literature on pastoral theology and method that addresses the African American context, this book acknowledges an urgent need to search for and explore new sources to aid in conceptualizing a framework for pastoral theology that is specific to the needs of Black people in America.

As a means to extrapolate the Black experience in America (short of an ethnographic or qualitative study), sources from the disciplines of systematic Black liberation theology, womanist theology, Black psychology, and African American literature will be examined in order to provide interpretations of African American experience. The implication is that cognate sources that are indigenous to the African American context most often offer more knowledge about the African American experience for theological reflection—as secondary resources—than the knowledge of many pastoral caregivers who function out of the traditional modality of pastoral theology and care.[15]

Finally, the correlation of African American sources will help to provide the basis for the conceptual framework for pastoral theology in the African American context. Chapters 2 through 6 demonstrate how knowledge of African American experience can be obtained through the examination and correlation of sources that are indigenous to the African American context.

Specifically, chapter 2 provides background information for the African American context in the form of a large case study on the collective experience of African Americans, past and present. A brief overview and analysis of African American history and a social analysis of the contemporary situation experienced by the majority of Black people sharing the social location of poor Black women in America will be presented.

The middle section of the book involves an examination of cognate sources. Chapter 3 presents an examination of African American theological sources, featuring the work of Black liberation theologian James H. Cone and womanist theologians Jacquelyn Grant and Delores S. Williams. Chapter 4 engages a discussion on Black psychology, featuring the thought of Black psychologists Wade Nobles, Arthur C. Jones, Molefi Asante, Linda James Myers, Kobi Kambon, and Nancy Boyd-Franklin. Chapter 5 introduces sources from the African American literary tradition as interpretive of the psychological experience of

---

[15] I am referring to those pastors and caregivers that rely more on their intellectual or traditional academic understandings to inform their experience of the ministry context rather than the actual experience of those living in ministry context.

African Americans. The work of African American authors Toni Morrison and James Baldwin will be featured. Throughout the examination of all the literature, ideas that are primarily of the womanist school of thought will be highlighted for their benefit to pastoral theological method for the African American context.

The final three chapters are more integrative in nature. Chapter 6 will correlate African American theology, Black psychology, and African American literature. Chapter 7 will present an appropriation of pastoral theology for African Americans, setting guidelines for the pastoral care of African Americans from a womanist perspective. Finally, chapter 8 discusses strategies for the survival and liberation of African Americans and for the transformation of American society.

CHAPTER 2

The African American Context

Prophetic thought must have the capacity to provide a broad and deep analytical grasp of the present in light of the past.

Cornel West

Historical Background of the African American Context

Just as traditional pastoral theology has been developed, primarily, from the European American perspective, until recent years the majority of American history has been interpreted and written from a European American worldview. Consequently, the average American knows relatively little about the subjective story of African people brought to this country as slaves. Therefore, this chapter will briefly revisit American history from the perspective of Africans brought to this country as slave labor and from the perspective of their descendants who experience subsequent subjugation and pervasive forms of personal, cultural, and institutional racism in contemporary times.

Described in the simplest terms, the history of African Americans has been one of oppression and resistance to oppression.[1] Historian Vincent Harding's book *There Is A River: The Black Struggle For Freedom in America* tells a story of American experience from the perspective of Black Americans engaged in a centuries-long "struggle for freedom and justice." As Harding focuses on the historical experience of Blacks, he effectively employs the metaphor of the steady stream of a river to emphasize "the ongoing movement of the black struggle" as part of the story within America's story.[2]

Built on a foundation of racism, the system of slavery in the Americas represents the cruelest form of slavery enacted in recent times. From the time my African ancestors boarded ships destined for the New World, they were engulfed by white racism in its harshest form—designed to strip these Black people of their rich African cultural heritage and of their humanity.[3] Integral to this racist system was a massive genocide of African people. African slaves had only two choices: slavery or extermination. While precautions were taken to keep slaves from escaping, none were taken to ensure their survival except attempts to deny them the choice of taking their own life rather than to be enslaved. Many died because of the insufferable conditions, were murdered as they resisted, or managed to commit suicide while en route to the Americas. It is estimated that 40 million Africans died at sea during transport—casualties that were allowed for—and only an approximate 20 million slaves actually reached their destinations.[4] Based on these estimations, of the 60 million Africans chosen for slavery, only a third of those survived the crossing of the Atlantic Ocean.

---

[1] I agree with Cornel West (and others) that the history of African Americans is more than a "history solely of oppression" or "solely of resistance" or "narrow views that we [as a people] have done nothing." See Cornel West, *Prophetic Reflections: Notes on Race and Power* (Monroe, Maine: Common Courage Press, 1993). However, my intent here is to focus on the nature of existential concerns for African Americans in a culture of oppression and, ultimately, the significance of these concerns for pastoral theological reflection.

[2] See Vincent Harding, *There is a River: The Struggle for Freedom in America* (New York: Vintage Books, 1981) for an expansive history of the Black freedom movement.

[3] Ibid., 6–8.

[4] Lerone Bennett, Jr., *Before The Mayflower* (Baltimore: Penquin Books, 1968), 30.

History clearly indicates that only the strong survived. Yet, for the most part, survival was not so much due to one's individual strength as it was a result of the collective support, resistance, and resilience of the slave community. Although the Africans were forced to let go of their language and many of their rituals, they held firmly to the African philosophy of life expressed in the African proverb: "I am because we are and because we are, therefore I am."[5] Thus, sticking together and taking care of one another proved to be the real strength of resistance. Networks of extended family and kinships continued to nurture and care for children who were orphaned by death and separation from parents on the auction block, offsetting the intended destruction of familial unity among the slaves.[6]

Initially, African forebears of the Black freedom movement struggled to not surrender their freedom to their captors, to not be taken from their homeland, to not have their families broken. Liberation was always the ultimate objective. However, in view of the brutal and cruel treatment received at the hands of their captors, survival became a prerequisite for liberation at some hoped-for future time.[7] To the present day, Black people have had to adjust to life within a culture of oppression while maintaining a resistance to the effects of that oppression.

Glimpses of History from the Perspective of Black Women

Within the story of African people in this country, there is also a history specific to Black women's experience that has largely been ignored by historians. This history is, of course, essential to an understanding of Black women's perspective on life in America and foundational to womanist thought in general. Thus, it is quite fitting to consider the specifics at various stages in American history from the worldview of Black women.

---

[5] Na'im Akbar, "Nile Valley Origins of The Science of Mind," *Nile Valley Civilizations,* ed. Ivan Van Sertima (New Brunswick, N.J.: Journal of African Civilizations, 1985), 130.

[6] Nancy Boyd-Franklin, *Black Families in Therapy: A Multisystems Approach* (New York: Guilford Press, 1989), 16.

[7] Ibid., 4–23.

In the introduction to her book *Labor of Love, Labor of Sorrow: Black Women, Work and the Family, From Slavery to the Present*, Jacqueline Jones points out that Black women belong to a "unique subculture, one not shared entirely with Black men or white women."[8] Black women's culture has a paradoxical nature: Their shared experience of slavery with Black men gave them a certain kind of parity with Black men, while there was extreme disparity between the experiences of Black women and White women at the same time.

On the one hand, Black women experienced and endured the same kinds of physical and psychological atrocities as Black men, because during slavery, racism was more pervasive for Black women than sexism. It is important to keep in mind that the slave masters' approach to their slave labor in this country was "gender-blind." Their priority was to get the highest possible production out of their slaves (male or female) without making any real distinctions between the sexes. Therefore, there was no preferential treatment for slave women. On the contrary, Black women had no choice but to produce to their maximum physical ability or suffer the same severity of punishment as their male counterparts. However, there were two major differences in the experience of Black women that set them apart from Black men: First, slave women had to be workers and childbearers at the same time; pregnancy was no excuse for lack of production. Second, female slaves were more susceptible to sexual abuse than males.[9]

On the other hand, gender has never been an adequate basis for making generalizations about the experiences of Black women and White women. Although both races of women held the possibility of motherhood in common, in reality, the differences in skin color set Black women and White women drastically apart in their experiences of womanhood. While slavery was a way of life in America, White women enjoyed the distinction and privilege of being "feminine" and, therefore, worthy of pampering and protection, while Black women were

---

[8] Jacqueline Jones, *Labor of Love, Labor of Sorrow: Black Women, Work and the Family, From Slavery to the Present* (New York: Vintage Books, 1985), 5.
[9] Ibid., 11–20.

despised and abused. White women themselves were every bit as racist as White men. Often, many slave women preferred field work to domestic work because of the abusive treatment they received at the hands of hateful White mistresses. Even though Black women were the nursemaids and caretakers of White women's households, their abuse at the hands of White women came not only as a result of White women's racism. The abuse also was related to the anger that many White women felt about their own abuse as women, and their jealousy toward slave women, who were very often the sexual objects of their husbands.[10]

Cognizant of the fact that Black women had always had to work as hard as any man in this country, without any regard for their femininity, abolitionist Sojourner Truth openly pondered this paradox of being Black and female by posing the question, "Ain't I a woman?" in an address given at a conference on women's rights in 1851. Sojourner Truth's question was for White men and women alike. Her words clarified the perspective of Black women who took time out from the larger struggle of Black people to fight for women's rights in general: Black women called for the country to address the race issue (abolition) alongside the sex issue (women's suffrage). More specifically, Sojourner Truth was also asking the White women in their fight for liberation to join the fight of their Black sisters against racism in the form of slavery. Unfortunately, history shows that White women who were so-called "abolitionists" continued to "discriminate against Black women." Because of their "differences," Black women and White women have not been able to come together effectively in either liberation struggle as a result.[11]

Black Women's Resistance

At every stage of the Black struggle for freedom, Black women have participated in every kind of resistance just as Black men have. Consistently, Black women have fulfilled a crucial

---

[10] Ibid., 20–28.
[11] Paula Giddings, *When and Where I Enter: The Impact of Black Women on Race and Sex in America* (New York: Bantam Books, 1984), 54–55.

role as they continued to adapt to the needs of the family and the community. As Black women fought and died alongside Black men, the wisdom of their unique culture provided for a kind of creativity and ingenuity that allowed them to formulate strategies that turned each challenging situation into an opportunity to advance their people's struggle.[12]

Womanist Katie Cannon writes about how a moral wisdom that was born of Black women's culture in this country empowered Black women to cope with the realities of White domination as they devoted themselves to the survival and liberation of Black people. In their family roles, Black women were usually the keepers of the African ancestors' cultural heritage. In turn, Black women appropriated the wisdom of their African foremothers to the circumstances of oppression in America and passed this wisdom on to their daughters and granddaughters to benefit the well-being of the Black community at large.[13]

Along the same lines, in their roles as wives and mothers, Black women were primarily responsible for the domestic duties and nurture of the Black family's life. Regardless of how or where Black women were positioned on plantations, whether in the fields or in the master's house, whatever action they took on behalf of the struggle was determined by how best they could keep their families intact. More often than Black men, Black women did not flee to freedom unless they could take their children with them. In other cases, Black women escaped to freedom along with Black men and formulated a plan for the whole family to follow.[14]

During the Civil War, in the absence of some 96,000 Black men who left the South to join the efforts of the Union army, Black women had to bear the heavy burdens of the transitional period between slavery and the actual emancipation of the slaves at the war's end. If ever there was a time when equating the Black woman to a mule seemed to ring true, as Zora Neale Hurston's character Nanny in her novel *Their Eyes Were Watching God* did, it was during this time period in American history:

---

[12] Harding, 12.

[13] See Katie G. Cannon, *Black Womanist Ethics* (Atlanta: Scholars Press, 1988).

[14] Jones, 46–48.

So de white man throw down de load and tell de nigger man tuh pick it up. He pick it up because he has to, but he don't tote it. He hand it to his women folks. De nigger woman is de mule uh de world so fur as Ah can see.[15]

Indeed, the metaphor of a mule or mules carrying the world portrays an image that vividly depicts the reality of Black women in this country while the Civil War was going on: Black women seemed to be carrying the whole country on their backs. In the absence of the men, Black women bore most of the burden of maintaining the plantations and their own families including the young, the old, and the sick. Inasmuch as Black women and their children remained behind the enemy lines of the Confederacy, they also had to bear the brunt of the bitter outrage of the Confederate Whites who surrounded them. Nonetheless, Black women resisted by slowing down in their work and defecting behind Union lines with their children whenever the opportunity arose.[16]

As time moved on, Black women were relentless in their efforts against racial oppression. During the period of Reconstruction following the Civil War, Black women continued to be innovative in their resistance. As mentioned earlier, Black women involved themselves in the White women's movement for women's suffrage for a time while they actively participated in every facet of organizing the Black political machine in the South. Of particular interest here, Black women were some of the first women to test Reconstruction legislation by making financial claims against their previous masters and current White lovers who kept them as mistresses and/or fathered children with them.[17]

Although Black women involved themselves in the so-called women's movement, it became clear that it was a movement for the advancement of the White women's agenda alone. Black women found it necessary to evolve their

---

[15] Zora Neale Hurston, *Their Eyes Were Watching God,* reprinted ed. (Urbana, Ill.: University of Illinois Press, 1978), 29.
[16] Jones, 46–51.
[17] Giddings, 64–74.

organizing efforts into a Black women's club movement, The National Association of Colored Women, apart from White women for two major reasons: First, the racism and classism of White women prevented them from incorporating the perspective of Black women into the agenda of the women's movement; second, Black women did not intend to separate themselves from the overall Black struggle they shared with Black men. Thus, Black women's clubs formed toward the end of the nineteenth century sustained the Black struggle up to the Civil Rights era. In fact, it was the anti-lynching campaigns that originated in the Black women's club movement that "launched the modern civil rights movement."[18]

The earliest stages of the twentieth-century so-called civil rights movement began at the grassroots levels of the Black community "in the rich tradition of protest." In turn, Black women worked in conjunction with the efforts of the Black church community and organizations such as the SCLC (Southern Christian Leadership Conference), the NAACP (National Association for the Advancement of Colored People), CORE (Congress of Racial Equality), and SNCC (Student Non-violent Coordinating Committee) to achieve equality for Black people.[19]

Clearly, the memory of Martin Luther King, Jr., symbolizes the accomplishments of the movement for most people. Many may also recall the key role that Rosa Parks played that fateful day in Montgomery, Alabama, when she refused to give up her seat in the front of the bus to move to the back. However, the role that Black women played in this movement remains largely untold.[20]

Rosa Parks's actions that day are indicative of the mood and attitude of resistance common to Black women living in the South at that time. Parks's arrest brought the media attention that catapulted Martin Luther King, Jr., into the limelight of the news media. Yet the truth of the matter is that these kinds

---

[18] Ibid., 85–94.

[19] See Aldon D. Morris, *The Origins of the Civil Rights Movement:Black Communities Organizing for Change* (New York: Freedom Press, 1984).

[20] For the most part the story is untold in written terms. We await written documentation of more of the history during the Civil Rights years in the stories of women who were very active during those years, such as Diane Nash, Prathia Wynn Hall, Zahorah Simmons, and others. However, the oral tradition is yet alive among many Black people, and in this instance primarily among Black women, through whom the stories of Black women are told.

of instances were happening throughout the South, where Blacks were expected to occupy the back of shared public places and to use separate public facilities from Whites. Often it was Black women who dared to confront the White establishment. Yet it was also common for Black women who were and are the backbone of the Black church to acquiesce to the usually male pastor's leadership in public matters. These Black women, domestics and students alike, who were primary and foundational to the efforts of the above-mentioned organizations, remained unacknowledged in the wake of Black male leadership. However, common sense tells us that Black women were a determining presence to the movement, as they had always been in the past.[21]

The Contemporary African American Context

Many gains were realized through the Black freedom movement during the 1960s, particularly some assurance of civil liberties under the law for all people in the public domain. Yet we witness in the present what Cornel West calls critical history: "the way the past has fundamentally shaped and molded the present."[22]

The current situation facing African Americans is indicative of the fact that the racist backlash has again effectively undermined the progress of the Black struggle. Collectively, the state of Black Americans in the final decade of the twentieth century is still quite critical. On the whole, African Americans have not been able to overcome the effects of systematic racism. Today the majority of African Americans live under conditions of genocidal poverty.[23] Systematic racism has prevented Blacks from being able to amass an economic base that would ensure that Blacks, as a people, are not disproportionately fill-

---

[21] Although there may be a written source that confirms these statements, this section comes out of the oral tradition of Black women's events of the civil rights movement.

[22] West, 204.

[23] What I am referring to as "genocidal poverty" is the kind of living conditions that are responsible for the growing death rate in the Black community. Although poverty is not normally listed as a cause of death, the malnutrition, fetal demise, untreated disease (due to lack of or poor health care), homicide, fratricide, suicide, and alcohol and drug abuse that are becoming prevalent in poor Black communities all contribute to the gradual form of genocide that has been integral to the systematic racial oppression of Blacks.

ing the prisons, unemployed, underemployed, undereducated, forced to comply with welfare systems, and living in ghettos as we currently are.

It is also becoming evident that the overall psychological well-being of African Americans has greatly diminished as Blacks seem to be losing an awareness of and access to the cultural heritage that sustained their African forefathers and foremothers throughout slavery.[24]

Apart from the scenes of despair within Black America is a separate reality for White Americans, many of whom live quite comfortably and securely on the inheritances that in many instances should have been handed down, at least in part, to the descendants of freed slaves. As it is, former African slaves were never adequately compensated for their labor, nor were any financial reparations of any kind ever granted for the unduly cruel treatment that Blacks received during their enslavement.[25]

Current statistical data substantiates the inequality of wealth that continues to exist between Blacks and Whites on the whole, indicative of the fact that the vast majority of African Americans have never been able to acquire a material base comparable to that of Whites. The National Urban League's presentation of statistics reflects a more accurate view from the perspective of African Americans than do government statistics.[26] Even though

---

[24] West, 204–5.

[25] African American oral history has it that freed slaves were promised forty acres and a mule as reparation for the cruelty of their unjust treatment along with the decree of emancipation. For the masses of Blacks nothing of this sort ever happened.

[26] The crux of the statistical data offered here is based on the time period most affected by the policies of the presidencies of Ronald Reagan and George Bush and has been compiled by the National Urban League for their publication *The State of Black America*. As African American historian Manning Marable stresses, the Reagan-Bush years began a revolution in American policy through which the social and economic inequity between Blacks and Whites (affecting health care, education, housing, etc.) grew. See Manning Marable, "Crossing Boundaries, Making Connections: The Politics of Race and Class in Urban America," *Speaking Truth to Power: Essays on Race, Resistance, and Radicalism* (Boulder, Colo.: Westview Press, 1996), 111. Even though the Clinton administration represents a line of New Democrats, partisan politics controlled by the Republican Conservative Right (as demonstrated by the movement to impeach President Clinton) indicate an intention of upholding the agenda that began during the Reagan and Bush era.

U.S. government statistics may reflect an overall increase in the numbers of African Americans who have reached middle-class status, the reality is that this increase has been slight, far too gradual, and too subject to the possibility of downturn in the future to give a true picture of what the masses of African Americans are facing. In 1991 the per capita net worth of Blacks was $8,967, as compared with $42,842 per capita net worth for Whites. The economic gains of a small percentage of Blacks who have acquired middle-class status economically in this country does not negate or justify the fact that large numbers of Black people exist at or under the poverty level.

The percentage of African Americans who have reached middle-class status is difficult to determine. Depending on who is compiling statistical data and what the parameters are that constitute what middle class is in terms of Black people, the numbers change frequently. A liberal estimate is that 28 percent of African Americans have reached middle-class status. Yet Black persons are often considered middle class by virtue of their level of education, even when their income does not compare with the income of middle-class Whites. According to the U. S. Department of Commerce, Bureau of the Census, in 1986, a glaring reality in the simplest terms is that the average White household had ten times more wealth than the average Black household, and the disparity was on the increase. [27] Economist David Swinton, writing about the period during and immediately following the Reagan-Bush presidential era, describes the stark contrast between the economic situations of Blacks and Whites:

> The latest data from 1991 and 1992 on income, poverty, and labor market status reveal a continuation of the disadvantaged status of blacks. The Reagan-Bush era closed as it began: with an economy gripped by recession or, at best, in a very anemic recovery. However, for African Americans, the entire period has been characterized by conditions that would be considered

---

[27]See Claud Anderson, *Black Labor, White Labor: The Search for Power and Economic Justice* (Edgewater, Md.: Duncan & Duncan, 1994), 33.

depression level if they were experienced by all
Americans.[28]

Swinton's statement begs the question, Why do the living conditions of Whites and Blacks, across the board, continue to be
so glaringly inequitable?

Many Americans seemingly choose to ignore the obvious
economic inequity between the two races in what is assumed
to be their denial that institutionalized racism still exists in this
day and age; many African Americans consciously acknowledge that they must continue to fight against the racial injustices at work within this country's structures. On the other hand,
many African Americans are aware of the truth of Swinton's
statement. They understand that, while economic downturns
have affected all Americans, the fact that African Americans
seem to absorb the brunt of the negative economic effects is no
accident.

Here it is important to note that many African Americans
believe that the response of this country's leadership to the growing competitive nature of the global economy (i.e., the conservative political agenda that was firmly reestablished during the
Reagan-Bush era) is more of the same; it is only a subtle form of
renewed racial oppression. Statistical data taken from the National Urban League's publication *The State of Black America 1993*
substantiates some of the economic disparity that exists between
Whites and African Americans in the final decade of the twentieth century. This data supports the idea that the agenda of the
Reagan-Bush era (1980–1992) invoked the power of institutional
racism, especially in labor and financial markets. Such political
maneuverings protected the status quo, while ensuring that African Americans would remain marginalized at the bottom of
this country's socioecomonic ladder.

---

[28] David H. Swinton, "The Economic Status of African Americans During
the Reagan-Bush Era: Withered Opportunities, Limited Outcomes, and Uncertain
Outlook," *The State of Black America 1993*, ed. Billy J. Tidwell (New York: National
Urban League, 1993), 135.

Economics of the United States' Labor and Financial Markets

From slavery through the industrial age and beyond, the free and low-cost physical labor of Black men and women—more so than any other racial group—undergirded this country's economy. Today, however, the economy depends more heavily on technology and requires a labor force that provides "intellectual muscle" rather than "physical muscle." Inasmuch as the vast majority of Blacks have not managed to keep pace with the market changes, the future outlook for African Americans is not sanguine.[29]

Any negative effects on the overall American economy are worsened for Blacks when racial injustice is part of the equation. In view of the current economic circumstances surrounding African Americans, there are at least three major reasons—all having to do with racial discrimination—that ensure that African Americans on the whole will not fare well economically in the future.

First, in terms of marketable skills, the overall educational achievement of African Americans places them at a disadvantage in the highly competitive job market. As of 1991, Blacks had a 53 percent higher dropout rate than Whites: Only 66.7 percent of African Americans had finished four years of high school, compared with 87.5 percent of Whites; 29 percent of Blacks had finished one year of college, compared with 46.3 percent of Whites; 11.5 percent of Blacks had finished four years or more of college, compared with 25.2 percent of Whites. Thus, the lower educational achievement levels of Blacks as a whole force most African Americans to remain dependent on, and overrepresented in, jobs with slower growth rates such as manufacturing or middle-managerial positions. For the most part, Blacks are underrepresented in the faster growing sectors that require technical knowledge.[30]

---

[29] Billy J. Tidwell, "African Americans and the 21st Century Labor Market: Improving the Fit," in *The State of Black America 1993*, ed. Billy J. Tidwell (New York: National Urban League, 1993), 35–38.

[30] Ibid., 43–51.

Second, in most job markets the advancement of technology has reduced the number of laborers required to accomplish the work. As a result, it has been determined that in recent years Blacks have more often been affected by corporate downsizing than Whites because in most instances they were the "last hired" and, therefore, the "first fired." For example, in comparison to Whites in the manufacturing industry, Blacks are 1.6 times more likely to become jobless, are less likely to be reemployed at all, and experience longer periods of unemployment than their White counterparts.[31]

A third factor in the American economy that works against the ability of Blacks to acquire a future economic base is the prevalent discrimination in the extension of credit within the country's financial institutions. For example, in terms of home loans, data from the Home Mortgage Disclosure Act (HMDA) substantiates the disparity in the rejection rates for loans between Blacks and Whites.

> HMDA data show that commercial banks and other lenders reject loan requests from black households at a higher rate than from white households at all income levels observed. In fact, the rejection rate of high-income black households is higher than the rejection rate of low-income white households. [32]

Low-income Whites, across the board, are more successful at acquiring home loans than Blacks of higher income brackets. Further, Blacks in general experience unequal treatment when it comes to selling their homes and getting a fair market price. There are also documented cases in which the appraised value of Black-owned homes or homes located within a predominantly Black community have often been devalued by as much as $15,000 of their fair market value.[33]

---

[31] Ibid., 43–52.

[32] William D. Bradford, "Money Matters: Lending Discrimination In African American Communities," in *The State of Black America 1993*, ed. Billy J. Tidwell (New York: National Urban League, 1993), 109.

[33] Ibid., 109–14.

Hopelessness and Despair in Black America

No doubt the realities of Blacks in the labor and financial markets exacerbate the life difficulties of Blacks. Yet deductive reasoning would conclude that there is a correlation between the depressive nature of the labor and financial markets for Blacks and the high rate of crime in the Black community. An excessively large percentage of Blacks occupy the country's prison systems, and there is a high mortality rate, especially among young Black men, due to homicide in one form or another (as a result of police brutality, gang warfare, Black-on-Black crime, etc.). In his study of the psychology of Black-on-Black crime, Black psychologist Amos Wilson reported the following statistics regarding crime among Black men:

> According to the Uniform Crime Report, published by the Federal Bureau of Investigation, in 1986 Blacks accounted for 45.5 percent of all arrests for violent crimes even though Blacks comprised only 12 percent of the U.S. population. Blacks accounted for 48 percent of the persons arrested for murder; 46 percent of all arrests for rape; 39.8 percent for assault. In the cities of the United States Blacks accounted for 49.5 percent of all arrests for violent crimes, for example, murder, forcible rape, robbery, and aggravated assault.[34]

The key words in Wilson's report about crime among Blacks are "arrests" and "arrested." The fact that Blacks experience a high percentage of arrests for crime is not necessarily indicative that Blacks are unequivocally responsible for nearly half of this nation's crime. The number of convictions for crimes resulting in incarcerations is another story.

In terms of those accused, arrested, convicted, and sentenced to prison terms and/or death row, it is ironic that racial injustice permeates the so-called "criminal justice system." The race of the accused is related to the final outcome once one enters the legal system. Michael Parenti makes a point in his book *Democracy for the Few* that compared with Whites, Blacks receive

---

[34] Amos N. Wilson, *Black-on-Black Violence* (New York: Afrikan World Infosystems, 1990), xi.

longer prison terms, and the number of executions of Blacks far outnumbers those of Whites for comparable crimes.

> Although many more whites than blacks have been convicted of murder over the last fifty years, over 53 percent of those executed have been black. The Law Enforcement Assistance Administration reports that between 1930 and 1979 a total of 1,754 whites and 2,066 blacks across the nation were executed, with 1,659 executions of blacks occurring in the South. In southern states, blacks were executed for murder more than twice as often as whites and an astounding nine times as often for rape. In 1984, 540 blacks sat on death row, 42 percent of all such inmates.[35]

As of 1989, the Bureau of Justice reports that of the total male population between the ages of 20 and 29 in the criminal justice system (those in jail, on probation, and on parole), 1,054,508 are White males (6.2 percent of White males in that age group), 609,690 are Black males (23 percent of Black males in that age group), and 238,255 are Hispanics males (10.4 percent of Hispanic males in that age group). The reality of what is going on with young Black males is quite glaring—nearly one of every four young Black males is involved in the criminal justice system.[36]

Moreover, the reality is all the more glaring when one considers that

> In 1986 African American men were about 6 percent of the American population, 3.5 percent of the college enrollment, and 46 percent of the prison population. By the year 2000, experts predict a 50 percent increase to at least 750,000 Black prisoners in the United States.[37]

Aside from the detriment to the well-being of the Black community, the true meaning of these figures is a disgrace to

---

[35] Michael Parenti in Rufus Burrow, Jr., "Black Males in Prison: The Silence of the Church," *Encounter*, 54.1 (Winter 1993): 42.

[36] Gayraud Wilmore, ed., *Black Men in Prison: The Response of the African American Church* (Atlanta: ITC Press, 1990), i.

[37] Ibid., 5.

American society: Prisons are warehouses for a large and disproportionate number of Black men, while America's institutions of higher learning only permit the attendance of a small percentage of Black men. In a context of racial parity this would not be the case. This contrast exemplifies the experience of far too many Blacks; it presents two extremes of institutionalized racism.

Earlier, the term *genocidal poverty* was introduced as an experience of many African Americans. Many are dying as a result of the conditions of their poverty. One significant factor in the high mortality rate in Black America is the Black-on-Black crime that has resulted as the frustration of ghetto life turns inward on the Black community itself. Wilson reports relevant findings along these lines:

> In 1986, of those persons under 18 years of age, Blacks accounted for 54.9 percent of those arrested for violent crimes. The highest violent crime rates are demonstrated by young Black males. More young Black men died from homicide in one year (1977) than died in ten years in the Vietnam War. Black men are six times as likely as White men to be murder victims. Murder is the fourth leading cause of death for Black males of age 20–29. Between the ages of 15 and 24 homicide is the leading cause of death among Black males. The odds of becoming a murder victim are less than one in twenty for Black males living in the city, between the ages 20 and 29. Most violent crimes (84 percent) against Blacks were committed by Black offenders.[38]

The violence done to young Black males, whether it is homicide or fratricide, has reached epidemic proportions, literally placing the survival of Blacks in jeopardy. It has been suggested that in light of the level of depravity and confinement of ghettoized living, a growing frustration level among those dwelling in the Black ghetto develops over time. Thus, the escalation of violent behavior acted out in gang warfare and Black-on-Black crime is quite predictable.

---

[38] Wilson, xi.

The fact that the larger society has allowed the circumstances that bring about the demise of so many Black youth and Blacks in general to continue indefinitely suggests that it condones the gradual genocide that is taking place in the Black community. Social ethicist Rufus Burrow aptly articulates the sentiment of many African Americans by raising this question:

> Is it no wonder that so many African Americans have concluded that their death is a necessary requirement of the continued existence of the ostensibly democratic socioeconomic and political system that exists in this nation?[39]

The African American perspective gives new meaning to the word genocide, although genocide—like discrimination—is difficult to prove. Nonetheless, the lack of activity to address the socioeconomic problems specific to the Black community can be viewed as a deliberate way to contribute to the extinction of a people; the method used does not have to be of an immediate nature.

In addition to the fact that "an African American male has a one in twenty-one chance of being murdered before he is 25 years of age," disease and drug abuse are also significant factors in the demise of Black males. In 1984, for example, 30 percent of those who died of drug abuse were Black men, and 35 percent of those who died of AIDS were Black men.[40] Again, the premise is that negative socioecomonic factors that continue to go unabated in Black America contribute to the large percentage of mortality rates among Black men due to disease and drug abuse.

. In the preceding pages, the contemporary experience of African Americans has been viewed primarily through the lens of the Black male worldview, and all too often the discourse stops there. However, the multidimensional social and economic burdens of poor Black women's experience portrays in a different way the magnitude and severity of the problems of Black life in America. Therefore, a brief look at the Black experience

---

[39] Rufus Burrow, Jr., "Black Males in Prison: The Silence of the Church," *Encounter* 54.1 (Winter 1993): 44.

[40] Wilmore, 6.

in America from the interpretive framework of Black women's experience follows.

The Contemporary View of Poor Black Women

These days there is much discussion about the need for budget cuts, and all too often the talk turns to welfare reform as the panacea for this nation's budget problems. Along with that discussion comes the attack on Black women, who as the heads of single-parent households rely disproportionately on public assistance.[41] It has been their apparent misfortune to be born Black and female in this country.

The most impoverished group of adults in America are Black women, who are deemed to be at least five times more impoverished than White males. At least "50 percent of older African American women are poor or near poor."[42] Black women earn the least when compared with White men, Black men, and White women, and how Black women fare economically in this society is directly related to the status of Black men.

The high rates of unemployment and underemployment of Black men, the large numbers of Black men incarcerated, and the high mortality rates among Black males, along with high rates of drug and alcohol abuse by Black men all contribute to a high rate of absenteeism of Black men from the Black household. Consequently, statistics show that currently 44 percent of Black families are single-parent households headed by Black females.[43]

How Black children fare in today's society is directly correlated to how Black women fare. Thus, it is not surprising to learn that Black children are the most economically disadvantaged group of children in America. During the span of one year (1982–1983), 71.5 percent of the Black children in single-parent homes headed by Black women lived at poverty level or below, as compared with 47.4 percent of the White children who lived in single-parent households headed by White women.[44]

---

[41] See Charles Murray, *Losing Ground: American Social Policy 1950–1980* (New York: Basic Books, 1984).

[42] Lynn C. Burbridge, "Toward Economic Self-Sufficiency: Independence Without Poverty," in *The State of Black America 1993* ed. Billy J. Tidwell (New York: National Urban League, 1993), 78.

[43] Ibid., 74.

[44] Ibid., 77.

Is it any wonder that a majority of poor Black women are forced to comply with welfare systems in order to provide for their children?

Yet conservative policy makers seem to have a weak will for racial justice and are willing to ignore the reality of the economics with which Blacks have to contend. Rather, the call is for welfare reform that reduces and limits the financial aid in the name of forcing poor Black women and other poor women to become independent. Addressing the dilemma that poor Black women face, Lynn Burbridge writes in an article for the National Urban League's annual inquiry into the state of Black America:

> Although the welfare system was originally designed to help women remain at home with their families whenever they were without a male breadwinner, this is no longer the case. Staying at home and raising one's children are not considered "real" work, and those who do so are often considered irresponsible and reckless, at least if they are poor. While many have appropriately criticized the hypocrisy of the conservatives who have insisted that welfare recipients work while extolling the virtues of remaining at home in the name of "family values" for white middle-class women, one cannot deny overall changing expectations regarding women and work. The irony, of course, is that African American women have historically had a much stronger attachment to the labor force than any other group of women and continue to work in great numbers, including those who are public assistance recipients.[45]

Blacks, particularly Black women in this instance, have not been given credit for their attempts to be self-sufficient. The real issue that Burbridge raises in her article is that self-sufficiency should not equate to poverty. Public policy makers need to find constructive ways to ensure that every ethnic group has the means to be economically independent without poverty.

---

[45] Ibid., 71.

The critical issues facing Black women are multidimensional and, therefore, complex. Also, to date, although they are subjects worthy of research, to my knowledge no scholarly studies have been completed on the nature and correlation of crimes for which Black women are arrested, convicted, and incarcerated. Neither, to my knowledge, has conclusive information been compiled and published on the numbers of Black women who are killed needlessly as a result of gang violence and Black-on-Black crime. However, it is a widely acknowledged fact that much of the "anger, rage, and despair" directed toward Blacks from other Blacks "is especially toward black women who are the most vulnerable in our society and in black communities."[46]

In terms of genocidal poverty, when gender and economics are considered, Black women (old and young) and their children (considering the above statistics on violence to young Black males) fare worse than Black men in many instances. Some Black children do not even get a chance at life. Malnutrition coupled with disease, drug and alcohol abuse, and the lack of resources for adequate health care certainly contribute to increased instances of fetal demise among Blacks.

Finally, cognizant of the psychological effects that were sure to result from the long-sustained struggle of Black women and Black men in this country, without any real hope for the future, Vincent Harding seems a visionary in the following statement:

> [C]onsidering the precarious terrain of our current lives, I am concerned about the one force that may surely stop the river: the self destructiveness and despair that overwhelm us when we no longer know our own course, no longer remember our origins.[47]

Harding was seeing clearly into the future to a time such as now, when African Americans would seem overwhelmed by the "lingering effects of Black history." Life within a market-centered culture daily reminds many Blacks of their poverty, and the bombardment of images and definitions throughout the media seem to have eradicated the values and pride of our

---

[46] Cornel West, *Race Matters* (Boston: Beacon Press, 1993), 18.
[47] Harding, xxiv.

origin from the memory of African Americans.[48] It now seems that Harding's forebodings are being fulfilled as nihilism undermines the ability of descendants of African slaves to be resilient and resistant in the face of the current life situations we experience in America. Today, one wonders how long the struggle for survival and liberation can continue without some evidence of hope for an immediate change or intervention in the circumstances of African Americans. We must develop new strategies for the survival and liberation of African Americans that strengthen and heal the Black psyche and help to transform American society as well.

---

[48] bell hooks, *Yearnings: Race, Gender, and Cultural Politics* (Boston: South End Press, 1990), 155–63; Cornel West, *Race Matters* (Boston: Beacon Press, 1993), 11–20; West, *Prophetic Reflections: Notes on Race and Power in America* (Monroe, Maine: Common Courage Press, 1993), 203–21.

CHAPTER 3

Theological Sources for an African American Pastoral Theology

There can be no comprehension of Black Theology without realizing that its existence comes from a community which looks back on its unique past, visualizes the reality of the future, and then makes decisions about possibilities in the present.

James H. Cone

There is a tradition which declares that God is at work in the experience of the Black woman. This tradition, in the context of the total Black experience, can provide data for the development of a wholistic Black theology.

Jacquelyn Grant

I have come to believe that theologians, in their attempts to talk to and about religious communities, ought to give readers some sense of their autobiographies. This can help an audience discern what leads the theologian to do the kind of theology she does.

Delores S. Williams

My own personal experience as an African American woman, along with my awareness of the history of African

Americans, informs my belief that the most critical issues for pastoral care of African Americans are *survival and liberation* issues. There are also many individual cases of African American women, children, and men whose stories (like my own) I could share to attest to the dire effects of genocidal poverty and the injustice of all kinds of oppression. However, this book is directed toward the collective experience of African Americans with an intent to avoid the individualistic trap of traditional pastoral theology, which appears to distract the field from developing communal approaches to its methodology.

Historically, the traditional theological conversation of Western Christian theology has not adequately served the theological dimensions of the human situation in the African American context. Consistent with the way Western Christianity was often used as a means of control over America's slaves and indigenous people, in more recent times the emphasis of traditional theological concepts tends to ignore the issues of the oppressed populations of the world. Is it any wonder, then, that traditional pastoral theology, which has been influenced by traditional Western theology, also seems to ignore the more critical issues of oppressed people?

Seward Hiltner presents a dialogue with traditional existential and process theologians in his book *Theological Dynamics*, which is consistent with his interdisciplinary style. This discourse is a good example of how the teachings and doctrines of traditional Western theology in relation to psychological dynamics have influenced pastoral theologians in general.[1] It is important to note that Hiltner's categories that introduce the traditional theological discourse are limited to *freedom, gratitude, trust, sickness, sexuality, community,* and *death.*[2] Notably, there is no category that addresses the communal *survival* issues of African Americans. Further, although Hiltner's first chapter, "Freedom and Destiny," has possibilities of at least touching on the concept of *liberation* for African Americans, it does so only in a superficial way. In terms of my definitions for liberation (freedom) and Hiltner's concepts of freedom

---

[1] Seward Hiltner, *Theological Dynamics* (Nashville: Abingdon Press, 1972).
[2] Ibid., 17.

(self-fulfillment, self-direction, and self-transcendence), clearly the meanings and understandings are, indeed, worlds apart. Granted, while there is loose agreement between what I define (in part) as *liberation*/freedom for African Americans, "the ability to self-determine," and Hiltner's discussion of freedom as "self-direction,"[3] there is clear distinction in our worldviews. Hiltner's chosen categories (informed by traditional theology) represent a male European American cultural perspective that is politically and economically secure. My perspective represents the culture of African Americans who are politically and economically oppressed. Even Hiltner acknowledges this distinction in his own words:

> [I]t must be admitted that the preoccupation of most of our theological forebears was on the point of what people do with their freedom of self-direction, not whether or not they have any.[4]

That is to say, traditional theology and consequently traditional pastoral theology does not deal with the questions of those without the freedom to "self-direct" or to "self-determine." Case in point: the African American context. The difference in the cultural experience and thought between European American culture and African American culture makes it nearly impossible for the dominant/traditional cultural perspective to pose the kinds of theological questions that adequately represent the worldview and exigencies of African Americans as a whole. Hence, an African American theological conversation is a prerequisite to the enterprise of constructing African American pastoral theology.

African American theology, commonly referred to as *Black theology*, emerged out of the written expressions of Black church leaders and Black scholars who were engaged in the Black power movement of the 1960s.[5] Interestingly, the articulations of these pastors, church leaders, and scholars were initially referred to as *pastoral theology* by some Black theologians because they

---

[3] Ibid., 24–31.

[4] Ibid., 27.

[5] James H. Cone and Gayraud S. Wilmore, eds. *Black Theology: A Documentary History, Volume One: 1966–1979*, 2d and rev. ed. (Maryknoll, N. Y.: Orbis Books, 1993), 15.

raised the serious nature of Black existence in this country to theological discussion while pointing toward strategies and solutions.[6]

However, as Black theology evolved over the years, two distinctive systematic approaches for doing theology have become prevalent in the African American context: Black liberation theology and womanist theology. The methodology of both approaches asserts the distinctive experience of African Americans as the point of departure for doing theology. Respectively, these theologies represent the African American male perspective, whose primary theme has been Black liberation from racial injustice, and the theological perspective voiced by African American women, which encompasses gender and class issues as well as racial oppression and whose theme is survival and liberation. The first three sections of this chapter will focus on select works of African American theologians James H. Cone, Jacquelyn Grant, and Delores S. Williams. The collective body of literature of these theologians is quite impressive, representing theological reflection on extensive research into the African American experience.

James H. Cone and Black Liberation Theology

James H. Cone's writings were seminal to the development of systematic Black theology. Initially, as a young scholar, Cone struggled for the words to articulate the Black power movement in theological terms. As time went on, it was Cone's persistent scholarship, more than that of any other Black theologian at the time, that helped to conceptualize Black theology in systematic terms.[7] Mindful of the fact that the average African American (in and outside of the church) has little knowledge of Cone or Black theology as an academic discipline,[8] and that many White theologians criticize Cone's thought without taking time to reflect upon it or utilize it, Rufus A. Burrow, Jr., wrote

---

[6] Gayraud S. Wilmore, "Black Theology and Pastoral Ministry: A Challenge to Ecumenical Renewal and Solidarity," in *The Pastor as Theologian*, eds. Earl E. Shelp and Ronald S. Sunderland (New York: Pilgrim Press, 1988), 32.

[7] See James H. Cone and Gayraud S. Wilmore, eds., *Black Theology: A Documentary History, 1966–1979* (Maryknoll, N.Y.: Orbis Books, 1979).

[8] James Henry Harris, "Black Church, Black Theology," in *The Christian Century*, June 13–20, 1990.

a volume titled *James H. Cone and Black Liberation Theology.* Throughout the volume, as Burrow interprets Cone's transitions over time, he acknowledges the magnitude of Cone's contributions and illustrates why African Americans and the academic community in general are, indeed, deeply indebted to Cone. Not only was Cone "the first to write in a systematic way and deliberate way on the subject of Black theology," but his groundbreaking work continues to inform and challenge the work of generations of Black theologians to follow.[9]

The important thing to remember about Cone, particularly in his earliest writings, is that he wrote mindful of the history of African Americans and the unacceptable conditions that the masses of African Americans continued to live with in the '60s. Cone, therefore, wrote with anger. Somehow he had to be able to articulate the realities of the Black freedom struggle as he involved himself in that struggle through his scholarship within the echelons of Western academe. A question that stayed with Cone during that time period was: How could I continue to allow my intellectual life to be consumed by the theological problems defined by people who had enslaved my grandparents?[10] Hence, in the introduction of his first book, *Black Theology and Black Power*, Cone wrote:

> This work, then, is written with a definite attitude, the attitude of an angry young man, disgusted with the oppression of black people in America and with the scholarly demand to be "objective" about it. Too many people have died, and too many people are on the verge of death. In fairness to my understanding of the truth, I cannot allow myself to engage a dispassionate, noncommitted debate on the status of black-white relations in America by assessing the pro and con of Black power. The scholarly demand for this kind of "objectivity" has come to mean being uninvolved or not taking sides.[11]

---

[9] Rufus A. Burrow, Jr., *James H. Cone and Black Liberation Theology* (Jefferson, N.C.: McFarland & Company, 1994), xvii.

[10] James H. Cone, *My Soul Looks Back* (Nashville: Abingdon Press, 1982), 43.

[11] James H. Cone, *Black Theology and Black Power* (New York: Seabury Press, 1969), 2.

True to himself, Cone intentionally involved his scholarship on the side of the Black struggle for survival, freedom, and power. Therefore, he wrote his first book in very harsh tones to "Whitey," as he asserted the concept of "Black power" squarely within Christian theology.[12]

Burrow, however, unmasks an underlying motive for Cone's writing *Black Theology and Black Power*, asserting that what was even more true of Cone was his need to express theologically the deeper meanings of his own existence as a Black man and those of his people.[13] Although Cone never clearly stated Black experience as a source for doing Black theology at that time, it is implied throughout the book.

Cone wrote from his gut based on what he knew the Black experience to be. His reason for analyzing Black power from a theological perspective had everything to do with what American Blacks had been experiencing as a people. Thus, his writing, from the very beginning, was always for his people more than for Whites.[14]

What does Cone say about the experience of African Americans in Black theology and Black power? Speaking directly to the concern of many Christian Whites about the violence that came with the cries of "Black power," Cone wrote about the conditions of Black people who lived with "White hatred" and "under White oppression." The experience was one of ghetto living, being insulted, ignored, dehumanized, and virtually "enslaved by White social structures."[15] Thus, Cone identified Black power with the experience of Black people and our need for empowerment through theological response. Cone's definition for Black power was as follows:

> Black power means black freedom, black self-determination, wherein black people no longer view themselves as without human dignity but as...human beings with the ability to carve out their own destiny.[16]

---

[12] Ibid., 5–30.

[13] Burrow, 60.

[14] Later Cone removes all doubt that he is writing to and for Black people. See James H. Cone, *My Soul Looks Back* (Nashville: Abingdon Press, 1982); and *For My People: Black Theology and the Black Church* (Maryknoll, N.Y.: Orbis Books, 1984).

[15] Cone, *Black Theology and Black Power*, 5–12.

[16] Ibid., 6.

According to Cone, the appropriate theological response was that Black power was "Christ's central message to twentieth-century America."[17] The ontological significance of Black skin color is carried over to Cone's second book, *A Black Theology of Liberation*. Cone chose liberation as his theme for his theoretical framework for Black theology.[18] Stated very explicitly in the introduction of this book, Cone's purpose was to write "for the Black community, not for whites." Yet he announced to the academy:

> It is the task of the Christian theologian to do theology, in light of the concreteness of human oppression as expressed in color, and to interpret for the oppressed the meaning of God's liberation in their community.[19]

Black experience heads Cone's list of sources for Black theology, followed by Black history, Black culture, revelation, scripture, and tradition. According to Cone,

> The black experience is existence in a system of white racism. The black person knows that a ghetto is the white way of saying that blacks are subhuman and only fit to live with rats. The black experience is police departments adding more recruits and buying more guns to provide "law and order," which means making a city safe for its white population. It is politicians telling blacks to cool it…The black experience is college administrators defining "quality" education in the light of white values. It is church bodies compromising on whether blacks are human. And because black theology is a product of that experience, it must talk about God in light of it. The purpose of Black theology is to make sense of black experience.[20]

Delivered in a different tone overall, Cone's description of the Black experience in *A Black Theology of Liberation* was

---

[17] Ibid., 1.
[18] James H. Cone, *A Black Theology of Liberation*, 2d ed. (Maryknoll, N.Y.: Orbis Books, 1986).
[19] Ibid., vii–viii.
[20] Ibid., 24.

nonetheless glaring in light of the realities that African Americans faced daily. The kinds of experiences that Cone names above, common for far too many African Americans, came as a result of White society's racial oppression. The source and the nature of the experience was what the vast majority of Black Americans needed to be liberated from. Black liberation theology, then, was necessary because "American white theology [had] not been involved in the struggle for black liberation." On the contrary, Cone points out that "American white theology," based on traditions endemic to white racism, has been a theology that has supported the established order of the status quo.[21]

For Cone, scripture and the Black struggle for liberation were the two norms for making theological sense of the Black experience.[22] To speak of and about God, mindful of African American experience and apart from the language of traditional Western theology, Cone's question became, How can we speak about God without being associated with the oppressors?[23] His answer was to speak of God as Black. Thus, God as Black symbolized God's identification with those who are oppressed (such as Black people in this country) and their struggle for liberation.[24] Cone employed two principles of hermeneutics to arrive at the conclusion that "knowing God means being on the side of the oppressed." The first principle acknowledged God's identification with the oppressed in scripture. The second principle, on the basis of the historical biblical account of God's identity with the oppressed, calls us to identify with the contemporary struggle of the oppressed. Clearly the struggle that Cone addressed to theology was the Black struggle for liberation.[25]

Cone's next two books, *The Spirituals and the Blues* and *God of the Oppressed,* are indicative of his efforts to address the criticism from other Black theologians that his style was more dependent on Western theological method than on Black

---

[21] Ibid., 4.
[22] Ibid., 36.
[23] Ibid., 56.
[24] Ibid., 63–64.
[25] Ibid., 57–65.

experience.[26] However, Burrow argues that Cone's original intent and purpose was always to make theological scholarship responsive to the Black experience in America.[27]

The purpose of *The Spirituals and the Blues* was to affirm what Cone already knew about Black experience, historically and personally, through other sources that spoke to the Black experience. Hence, he sought "to examine the statement of Black experience," past and present, in Black music known as spirituals and blues.[28] His method was to make theological and historical comparisons between the spirituals and the blues. The spirituals were representative of the historical experience of Blacks during slavery in particular. And the early development of the blues is more representative of contemporary Black experience.[29]

Cone's research produced a rich resource for theological reflection. After a good deal of reflection upon the nature of their existence, he illustrated how the spirituals and blues sung by African Americans were deep expressions of the Black experience. Following are examples of powerful lyrics inspired by Black folks in the midst of trials and tribulations as they held out for "a brighter coming day." From the genre of the spirituals:

Song #1

> *Oh Freedom! Oh Freedom!*
> *Oh Freedom, I love thee!*
> *And before I'll be a slave,*
> *I'll be buried in my grave,*
> *And go home to my Lord and be free.*[30]

---

[26] Cecil Cone (brother of James Cone) eventually wrote a book on the subject of what he considered an "identity crisis" among Black scholars who were imposing Western theological constructs onto the Black context. See Cecil W. Cone, *The Identity Crisis in Black Theology* (Nashville: The African Methodist Episcopal Church, 1975). Others who criticized Cone were Gayraud Wilmore and J. Deotis Roberts et al.

[27] Burrow, 106.

[28] James H. Cone, *The Spirituals and the Blues* (New York: Seabury Press, 1972), preface.

[29] Ibid., 7.

[30] Ibid., 30.

Song #2

Nobody knows the trouble I've seen,
Nobody knows my sorrow.
Nobody knows the trouble I've seen, Glory, Hallelujah! [31]

Song #3

Soon-a-will be done with the trouble of the world,
Soon-a-will be done with the trouble of the world,
Going home to live with God. [32]

From the genre of the blues:

Song #1

Well, the blues ain't nothin'
But a working man feelin' bad.
Well, it's one of the worst old feelin's
That any poor man's ever had. [33]

Song #2

Times is so tough, can't even get a dime,
Yes times is so tough, can't even get a dime,
Times don't get better, I'm going to lose my mind. [34]

Song #3

Now, if you're white
You're all right,
If you are brown,
Stick aroun'
But if you are black,
Git back! Git back! Git back! [35]

The spirituals and the blues have been sung by Black people on the North American continent to this day to soothe our minds and souls and to tell our stories, past and present. The above descriptive lyrics are not unlike the words of Cone's personal interpretations of Black experience. Clearly, Cone's theme of

---

[31] Ibid., 63.
[32] Ibid., 64.
[33] Ibid., 122.
[34] Ibid., 123.
[35] Ibid., 126.

liberation is also quite significant throughout the music of the spirituals and the blues. Is it any wonder that Cone would say, "I, therefore, write about the spirituals and the blues, because *I am the blues and my life is a spiritual.*"[36]

The thesis of *God of the Oppressed* was that all theology is conditioned by the historical and social context of a particular people.[37] Cone boldly asserts that theological "sources must include the history and culture of oppressed people." In terms of Black people, Cone adds that, "[H]ere the Theologian asks: How have Black people understood their history and culture, and how is that understanding related to their faith in Jesus Christ?" According to Cone, the place to go for answers is the "black sermon, prayer, song, and story," which all relate understandings of the Black experience in America.[38]

Jacquelyn Grant and Black Women's Theology

Jacquelyn Grant, who is also an ordained elder in the AME Church, is considered a leading *first generation* womanist theologian. Her writings on the theological perspective of Black women precede the adoption and appropriation of the *womanist* nomenclature in the scholarship of African American women.[39]

Grant's article "Black Theology and the Black Woman" focuses on the difference of experience between Black men and Black women not only within American society but, primarily, in the Black church and in the academy of religious scholarship. In essence, Grant agrees with the premise of Black male theologians that Black experience is the appropriate point of departure for theological reflection, and, consequently, the theme of liberation. However, Grant's intent, as a Black woman scholar, was to criticize the theology of Black men (up to this particular point in time) for its failure to address the totality of Black experience. Therefore, Grant argues that in much the same way that White theologians had not taken the specifics of Black

---

[36] Ibid., 7.
[37] James H. Cone, *God of the Oppressed* (New York: Seabury Press, 1975), 15.
[38] Ibid., 10.
[39] Following the introduction of Alice Walker's term *womanist* in 1983, African American women religious scholars adopted the term and began to appropriate the four-part definition as methodological framework for their work. See Katie Geneva Cannon, *Katie's Canon: Womanism and the Soul of the Black Community* (New York: Continuum, 1995), 24.

experience in America into consideration, Black male theologians had failed to consider the specifics of the kinds of oppression experienced by Black women.[40]

Grant raises the issue for the field of Black theology that oppression for Black women is far more complex than that of Black men. It is multidimensional—having to do with racism, sexism (including the "peculiar kind oppression" of Black women that Black men must take responsibility for), and classism.[41] In addition to the sexism endemic in American society in general, Grant implies that Black male leaders must take responsibility for the invisibility of Black women in theology and leadership roles in the Black church, as well as in the Black community at large. Grant says that this behavior on the part of Black men is indicative of a "conspiracy to keep women relegated to the background."[42] Therefore, she responsibly confronts Black males in these arenas for their complicity with the evil oppression of sexism against Black women.[43]

At this point it is instructive to note that although Grant's intent is to focus Black theology on the experience of Black women, she appears to indirectly touch on psychological issues connected with the oppression of Blacks in general. (Chapter 4 of this book addresses the psychological experience of African Americans exclusively. However, Grant's discussion here serves to shed some light on the psychological experience of Blacks as a result of their oppression.)[44] For example, in terms of the psychology of Black theologians, church leaders, and many other Black men, Grant accounts for their sexism as an apparent acceptance "without questioning the patriarchal structures of the

---

[40] See Jacquelyn Grant, "Black Theology and the Black Woman," in *Black Theology: A Documentary History, Volume One 1966–1979*, ed. James H. Cone and Gayraud Wilmore, 2d and rev. ed. (Maryknoll, N.Y.: Orbis Books, 1993), 323–38.

[41] Ibid., 323–24.

[42] Ibid., 328.

[43] Ibid., 325–31.

[44] There is a void in the literature of Black psychology that pertains to the effects of oppression. Recently, in the search for sources, Black scholars have begun to recognize the resource that Black theology is for interpreting the Black experience. For example, Dr. Lee H. Butler of Chicago Theological Seminary presented an unpublished paper, "Liberating Our Dignity, Saving Our Souls: Black Theology as a Resource of African American Pastoral Psychology," at the annual meeting of the American Academy of Religion, November 1997, San Fransisco.

White society as normative for the Black community."[45] In other words, "the concept of male control and supremacy" (pervasive in Western culture) was/is integral to their sense of psychological well-being.[46] In psychological terms of Black women, many of the layers and degrees of oppression unique to us are, indeed, quite negative. Grant states that sexual oppression of Black women "at the hands of Black men" is a "peculiar kind of oppression."[47] In reality, the "peculiarity" of oppression perpetuated by Black men (whose forefathers were cosufferers with Black women throughout slavery and who continue to experience the oppression of racial injustice) must present psychological problems difficult for some Black women to reconcile in their minds.

Along the same lines, Grant raises the issue of stereotypes of Blacks and how they affect the experience of Black women differently than Black men. Again, the added dimension of sexism, and the complicity of Black men as they adopt the sexist attitudes of "White male-dominated society," is hard for Black women to come to terms with.

> There are oppressive realities in the Black community which are related to, but not independent of, the fact of racism. Sexism is one such reality. Black men seek to liberate themselves from racial stereotypes and conditions of oppression without giving due attention to the stereotypes and oppressions against women that parallel those against Blacks. Blacks fight to be free of the stereotype that all Blacks are dirty and ugly, or that Black represents evil and darkness. The slogan of "Black is Beautiful" was a counterattack on these stereotypes. The parallel for women is the history of women as "unclean" especially during menstruation and after childbirth. Because the model of beauty in the White male-dominated society is the "long-haired blonde," with all that goes along with the mystique, Black women have an additional problem with the Western idea of

---

[45] Ibid., 326.
[46] Ibid.
[47] Ibid., 327.

"ugliness," particularly as they encounter Black men who have adopted this White model of beauty. Similarly, the Christian teaching that woman is responsible for the fall of **mankind** and is, therefore, the source of evil has had a detrimental effect on the experience of Black woman.[48]

Grant's argument is clear that to be both Black and woman is to experience life differently from Black men. In terms of the class issues, she also presents sociological data that supports an awareness that Black women experience themselves as the "poorest of the poor" and the "most oppressed of the oppressed." Thus, Grant's contention is that the experience of Black women "provides a most fruitful context for doing Black theology."[49]

Black women's experience as a source for theological reflection continued to be the subject of Grant's writing as she moved toward the construction of systematic theology from the perspective of Black women. In a chapter titled "Womanist Theology: Black Women's Experience as a Source for Doing Theology, With Special Reference to Christology," Grant's discussion centered on a critique of feminist theology. Basically, Grant argues that no more than classical theologians could assume to speak to the experience of Blacks and women, or Black male theologians could assume to speak for Black women, could White women assume that their perspective was adequate for the theological expressions of Black women's experience either.[50]

At this point, owning Alice Walker's term of *womanist*, Grant identifies womanists from the historical tradition of famous Black women. Based on facts from the lives of women such as Sojourner Truth, Jarena Lee, Ida B. Wells, and others, Grant states:

---

[48] Ibid., 327.

[49] Ibid., 332.

[50] See Jacquelyn Grant, "Womanist Theology: Black Women's Experience as a Source for Doing Theology, With Special Reference to Christology," in *Black Theology: A Documentary History, Volume Two, 1980–1992*, ed. James H. Cone and Gayraud S. Wilmore (Maryknoll, N.Y.: Orbis Books, 1993).

A womanist then is a strong Black woman who has
sometimes been mislabeled as a domineering castrating
matriarch. A womanist is one who has developed
survival strategies in spite of the oppression of her race
and sex in order to save her family and her people...
[W]omanist just means being and acting out who you
are and interpreting that reality for yourself.[51]

Thus, to do womanist theology would be to interpret the experience of Black women theologically as it truly is: representative
of the strongest as well as the poorest Black women and their
struggles against racism, sexism, and classism.

In addition to the historical narratives of strong Black women,
Grant relied on biblical interpretation and prayers of Black women
to glean their experience and understanding of God. These sources
revealed the womanist tradition: strong Black women's ways of
appropriating the distortions of their oppressor's culture and
strategizing for the survival and liberation of Black people. A
womanist interpretation of scripture dispelled the White interpretation of scripture. Black women's experiences gave new meaning to God, known as "creator, sustainer, comforter, and liberator."
Black women's experience also affirmed that Jesus as "divine
cosufferer" identified with their suffering.[52]

Christology has also been a focus of Grant's theological
constructions. In a her groundbreaking work *White Women's Christ
and Black Women's Jesus: Feminist Christology and Womanist Responses*, Grant does a more in-depth study and critique of Feminist theology, focusing on christological issues for women.[53] For
the purposes of this book, Grant's womanist response to feminist
christology is emphasized over her examination of the various
approaches to White feminist christology.[54] As mentioned earlier,

---

[51] Ibid., 278.

[52] Ibid., 278–81.

[53] See Jacquelyn Grant, *White Women's Christ and Black Women's Jesus: Feminist Theology and Womanist Response* (Atlanta: Scholars Press, 1989).

[54] Space does not allow a sidetrack into the examination of other sources not indig-
enous to the African American context (such as Feminist theology). However, Grant's
volume includes an extensive examination of White Feminist Christology. In terms of
Feminist Biblical Christology, Grant's primary analysis is of the contributions of Virginia
Mollenkott, Nancy Hardesty, and Letha Scanzoni. In terms of Liberation Feminist
Christology, Grant analyzes Letty Russell and Rosemary Radford Ruether. In terms of the
Rejectionist Feminist Perspective, Grant analyzes the work of Mary Daly.

my main objective is to illustrate that knowledge about the experience of Black women can be gleaned from theological sources indigenous to the African American context.

Grant's critique of feminist christology expands upon the distinct characterization of Black women's experience for theological reflection. It is important to note that the genesis of Grant's contextual study, apart from a desire to inform herself more about feminist constructions of christology, came from her personal awareness that Black women's religious experience interprets christology as "both oppressive and liberating." Grant's awareness came from being a Black woman who was raised in the culture of the Black religious tradition.[55] Whereas White feminist theologians present Jesus as a "feminist" (a biblical model of mutuality),[56] in nontraditional ways such as "Sister" and "Mary Magdalene,"[57] or as no model at all for christology,[58] Grant was aware of the need for womanist christology to acknowledge a history of poor Black women that affirmed the second person of the trinity as a "divine cosufferer," one who suffered as they did, but also suffered with them.

The basis of Grant's critique of White feminist christology was, then, that Jesus identified himself with the "least" (Mt. 25:34ff.). This was what was liberating about traditional christology in spite of Jesus' maleness. Yet, in reality, the work of white middle-class women theologians did not show evidence of their being identified with the "least" (poor Black women). Therefore, White feminist christology was not wholly liberating for Black women.

The final chapter of Grant's book is devoted to the womanist response to feminist christology. It relies on a wealth of historical

---

[55] Ibid., preface.

[56] Ibid., 109. The approach of biblical feminists did not deal with oppression in terms other than sexism. The concepts of "feminist," "nonconformist," "mutuality," and so on are presented to eliminate sexism.

[57] Ibid., 145. Liberation feminist theologians' approach also considered other kinds of oppression in a limited way, but the liberation of women's oppression was still primary. New imagery was the "primary source for doing theology."

[58] Ibid., 170. The rejectionist feminist perspective asks the question, Does it make sense for women to adhere to a religious tradition that enslaves women? Racism is subsumed in sexism.

data ("speeches, biographies, writings") on the experience of Black women. Grant's frame of reference interprets the experience of Black women during the period of slavery in this country and of Black women who served as domestics following slavery.[59] These sources conclusively reveal that Black women's experience as slaves and ex-slaves has been worlds apart from that of White women (as the historical data in chapter 2 confirms). During slavery, regardless of the sexism, White women enjoyed "the protection of White patriarchy" and were the oppressors just as White men were. Black women treated as animals had to withstand physical and psychological abuse at the hands of their White slave masters—male and female. Following slavery, the violence and abuse continued, and, for the most part, Black women continued in domestic service to Whites and were subordinate to White women in all kinds of social relations.[60]

In more contemporary times, Grant's critique of White feminist theology serves to speak to another dimension of Black women's experience. Specifically, Black women have experienced the condescension and the imposition of the White women's movement. The rhetoric of White women has often presumed to speak for and to impose their perspective on Black women. A classic example is demonstrated by Grant's response to feminist theologian Rosemary Radford Ruether's critique of the Black freedom movement and the Black church:

> One wonders…if even liberationist feminists are able to understand the particularity of non-white women's experience. This is reflected at two points. (1) Whereas Ruether correctly critiques the Black nationalist movement and the Black church for its lack of sex and class analysis, she incorrectly locates the tension between Black churches and the women's movement at the point of sexism of Black men. One could argue that the Black men's response to the women's movement is due equally to the racism of the women's movement as to

---

[59] Ibid., 6.
[60] Ibid., 196–99.

the sexism in the Black movement. There is no reason
to believe, as Ruether seems to make it appear, that
White women are more concerned about Black women
and the Black lower classes than are Black men...(2)
Ruether suggests that perhaps a better model for women
would be Mary Magdalene rather than Jesus...[T]here
is little reason to believe that a White woman salvific
model would be any more liberating of Black women
than a White male model.[61]

Apparently, Ruether presumes to speak on behalf of Black
women, implying that it is the sexism of Black men and their
consequent sexist oppression of Black women that has prevented
Black women along with Black men from supporting the
women's movement. In other words, Black men have controlled
Black women's response to the woman's movement. Grant's
hypothetical response for Black men can definitely be argued
from the point of view of Black women themselves. Given the
choice, Black women considered societal racism (which includes
the racism of White women) a more pervasive kind of oppression than societal sexism and/or the sexism of Black men. Therefore, Black women were, overall, more supportive of the Black
movement than the women's movement.

Thus, according to Grant, a major flaw of White feminist
theology was that white middle-class women had "presumed
universality of women's experience"—arguing the issue of sexism, to the exclusion of the racism and classism suffered by Black
women and the majority of women in the world who are non-
White.[62] In short, Grant asserts that White feminist christology
(theology) is inadequate for Black women because "it is White
and racist." First, it is White because it appeals to the experience of White women and its sources are those of White culture. Secondly, it is racist because White women "have accepted
and participated in the racism of the larger American society."[63]
Thus, White women could not presume to speak for Black
women. In the final analysis, the significance of Grant's work

---

[61] Ibid., 146.
[62] Ibid., 6.
[63] Ibid., 195–201.

for this book is that her own personal awareness, knowledge and use of historical data of Black women's phenomena, and faith experiences inspired her work. It is Black women's experience that raises the issues of sexism and classism, along with racism. It is also Black women's experience that dictated the need for womanist christology to embrace Black women's interpretation of the second person of the trinity as Jesus the Christ—one who identified himself with their *survival and liberation.*

Delores S. Williams and Womanist Theology

The work of womanist theologian Delores S. Williams reflects careful attention to the womanist tradition in doing theology. By this time in the literature of Black theology, *experience* as the point of departure has been firmly established. For womanist theology, specifically, Black women's experience is clearly the starting point for doing theology. In a chapter titled "Womanist Theology: Black Women's Voices," Williams articulates what it means in the womanist tradition for Black women to claim their voices in doing theology.[64] Consistent with the intentionality of Black women religious scholars to appropriate Alice Walker's definition of *womanist* in their methodology, this article affirms the usefulness of the definition to the construction of womanist theology. Inasmuch as the womanist tradition is evidenced in the history, religion, and culture of Black women, Williams asserts that it is the work of the womanist theologian to "search for the voices, actions, opinions, experience, and faith" of Black women. Thus, Williams' premise is that Walker's definition provides helpful clues for identifying the womanist tradition in Black women's experience.[65]

Focusing on part two of Walker's definition (the same portion mentioned in chapter 1), Williams emphasizes the exchange of conversation between a mother and daughter. Identified in this exchange are cultural codes of Black women that are specific

---

[64] See Delores S. Williams, "Womanist Theology: Black Women's Voices," in *Black Theology: A Documentary History, Volume Two, 1980–1992,* ed. James H. Cone and Gayraud S. Wilmore (Maryknoll, N.Y.: Orbis Books, 1993), 265–72.
[65] Ibid., 267.

to the womanist tradition. According to Williams this mother/ daughter conversation defines Black women of the womanist tradition as affirming of female culture, affirming and accepting of the variety of skin colors among Black people and among freedom fighters. Other clues inherent in the rest of Walker's definition describe womanists as motherers and nurturers, respecters of sexual preference, builders of community with Black women and Black men, strategists and co-laborers with Black men for the "survival and wholeness of an entire people," and lovers of the "Spirit" (God). The importance of Walker's definition for womanist theology, and ultimately African American pastoral theology, is the interpretation of "Who God is" as influenced by any of these attributes found in Black women's experience.[66]

In her book *Sisters in the Wilderness: The Challenge of Womanist God Talk*, Williams, in her own right, corroborates many of Grant's assertions about Black women's experience in the Black church and society and also speaks to the inadequacies of Black liberation theology and White feminist theology for Black women's experience. Williams provides a lengthy definition of womanist theology that appears to incorporate the fullness of Walker's definition of womanist in theological terms:

> [A] theological corrective [which] is developing that has considerable potential for bringing black women's experience into theology so that black women will see the need to transform the sexist character of the churches and their theology...Womanist theology is a prophetic voice...concerned about the well-being of the entire African American community, female and male, adults and children...Womanist theology attempts to help black women to see, affirm and have confidence in the importance of their experience and faith for determining the character of the Christian religion in the African American community. Womanist theology challenges all oppressive forces impeding black women's struggle for survival and for the development of a positive,

---

[66] Williams, "Womanist Theology," 265–72.

productive quality of life conducive to women's and the family's freedom and well-being. Womanist theology opposes all oppression based on race, sex, class, sexual preference, physical disability and caste.[67]

The specifics of Williams' method combines African American biblical interpretation, the motherhood and nurturing attributes of African and African American women, and the womanist tradition of "survival and wholeness of an entire people" as the specific basis for her construction of womanist theology.[68]

On the basis of the female-centered tradition of Black women's reading of the Bible, Williams selects the biblical story of Hagar (Genesis 16) because she realized "striking similarities between Hagar's story and the story of African American women" (Hagar was a slave woman of African descent).[69] Williams concluded theologically from the biblical story that God did not liberate Hagar and her son, Ishmael (when Abraham sent them into the wilderness to appease Sarah), but rather God helped them to survive in the wilderness.[70] Hence, Williams named her appropriation "the survival/quality-of-life" tradition of African American biblical appropriation.[71]

According to Williams, the importance of the Biblical story of Hagar and her son, Ishmael, is that it renders an interpretation from an African American perspective that parallels the lives of a majority of Black women and their children in America past and present. Williams states:

> I selected from Hagar's story those issues that had, simultaneously, personal, social, and religious significance for black women and for the African American community; the predicament of motherhood; the

---

[67] Delores S. Williams, *Sisters in the Wilderness* (Maryknoll, N.Y.: Orbis Books, 1993), xiii–xiv.

[68] Ibid., 1–12.

[69] Ibid., 3.

[70] This is an important distinction for womanist theology. Black liberation theology touched on "survival" as an issue for theology, but more so in terms of "identity" than anything else, and, of course, "liberation" was the emphasis for theological reflection. See James H. Cone, *A Black Theology of Liberation*, 10–17.

[71] Williams, 1–12.

character of surrogacy; the problem of ethnicity; the meaning and significance of wilderness experience for women and for the community.[72]

Paramount for Williams is the need to survive the wilderness experience until liberation comes.

So what are some of the analogies between the story of Hagar (the Egyptian slave woman) and the women of African descent in America? As already mentioned, Williams focuses on the issues of motherhood as they pertained to Hagar and African American women past and present. A brief account of the biblical story of Hagar and Ishmael (Gen. 16:1–6) is as follows: Hagar (an Egyptian slave girl), as Sarah's personal property, is forced to become a surrogate mother for Sarah. Thus, she is forced to have sexual relations with Sarah's husband, Abraham, and to become pregnant, to bear a child, and to care for the child. Ultimately, the oppressive conditions at the hands of her mistress, Sarah, are so unbearable for Hagar that she runs away. Yet upon the encouragement of God (or a messenger of God) and without a way to survive, she returns to her masters. Once Hagar's son Ishmael is born, her mistress' cruelty increases. Finally, once Sarah becomes the biological mother of a son, Isaac, Hagar and her son are forced out into the wilderness. Although Hagar and her son near their deaths, God is present with them and helps them to survive and ultimately to prosper. God promises that Ishmael's descendants will be numerous.

Similar to the account of African American women's experience presented in the historical and sociological data of chapter 2, Williams brilliantly focuses her attention on what she calls Black women's "re/production history." This approach to the history of Black women deals specifically with the issues of motherhood for Black women during and after slavery.[73] According to Williams,

---

[72] Ibid., 8.

[73] Williams uses the term *re/production history* to denote the focus on the politics of Black women's reproduction pointing to slavery issues of rape, breeding, surrogacy, and issues of domestic service to the dominant culture following slavery.

The African American community has taken to heart Hagar's story unto itself. Hagar has "spoken" to generation after generation of black women because her story has been validated as true by the suffering of black people. She and Ishmael together, as family, model many black American families in which a lone mother struggles to hold the family together in spite of the poverty to which ruling class economics consign it. Hagar, like many black women, goes into the wide world to make a living for herself and her child, with only God by her side.[74]

Like Hagar, African American women have been enslaved, their bodies controlled by their masters (raped and bred); they have been forced to provide care and nurture not only for their own children, but to the masters and their children; they have been poverty stricken, homeless, and often alone making a way for themselves and their children. Therefore, the striking analogies between the biblical account of Hagar and Ishmael and the historical account of African American women and people in general is referred to by Williams as a "wilderness experience."[75]

In the terms of womanist "loves Spirit" in Alice Walker's definition, Williams expounds on the God-talk of womanists, differentiating it from the God-talk of Black liberation theology and feminist theology. God in womanist theology is characterized as more than a "liberator" in the sense that the term has been appropriated in Black liberation theology or White feminist theology. Williams asserts that the experience of Black women does not accommodate itself solely to the Black liberation theology hermeneutic of the exodus story of the Hebrews. The story of Hagar is about slavery as experienced by a non-Hebrew female slave woman who was not liberated from her oppression, but sustained by God in the midst of a wilderness experience.[76] Neither does the experience of Black women

---

[74] Ibid., 33.
[75] Ibid., 158.
[76] Ibid., 144–49.

accommodate itself to the models and images of femininity in White feminist theological construction.

Thus, womanist theology has a responsibility to interpret and reflect upon the complexity of Black women's oppression and their ability to survive that oppression.[77] Williams says that womanist theologians must ask the question, What is God's word about survival and quality of life formation for oppressed and quasi-free people struggling to build community in the wilderness?[78] For Black women in America (devoted mothers and nurturers in the midst of the wilderness experience), the reality of the wilderness experience reflects an absolute dependence on the concept that "God is able" to make a way for them in the wilderness.[79]

Significant for the purpose of this book is Williams' awareness of Black women's experience (personal and historical) in North America, which inspired her to search the scriptures for analogies to the experience of poor Black women. The story of Hagar lends to the conceptual basis for a theological dialogue that allows for the issue of survival and quality living along with liberation. Williams' method also, along with Grant's and Cone's, affirms the search for sources that contain information about the historical experience of African Americans.

Conclusion

Notably, the methods that Black religious scholars used to extrapolate the Black experience recover historical and sociological data as well as cultural information, which includes knowledge of Black religious tradition and African American music known as spirituals and the blues. Theological reflection on their own personal knowledge of African American cultural experience (past and present), cultural sources, and relevant scripture was the basis for posing the theological questions and developing a theological response to the cultural oppression of African Americans. Clearly, Black theology affirms the need for pastoral theology to address the *survival and liberation* needs of

---

[77] Ibid., 201–2.
[78] Ibid., 161.
[79] Ibid., 108–39.

African Americans. Its content and methods are also useful for the construction of an African American pastoral theology. Further implications of African American theology for the construction of African American pastoral theology will be discussed in detail in chapter 6 along with the implications of Black psychology and the correlation of both fields. The next chapter reviews select sources in Black psychology for the purpose of interpreting the psychological experience of African Americans.

CHAPTER 4

Psychological Sources
for an African American
Pastoral Theology

*The psychology of a culture is to a great extent a symbolic
precipitant of the kinds of experiences forced upon a group
of people by their history. We must recognize the intimate
relationship between culture, history, and personality.*

Amos N. Wilson

Up to this point, the historical, sociological, and theological
implications of Black experience have been discussed in terms
of the physical elements of African American life (or oppression that is external) that create the need for *survival and liberation*. However, the psychological elements that have to do with
the inner experience of African Americans have not been addressed. This chapter will focus on the psychical experience of
African Americans. In terms of survival and liberation, the
premise is that there are negative psychological effects that are
residual from slavocracy's brutalization as well as deep psychological burdens for many African Americans as a result of
the traumas of contemporary life in American society. Inasmuch
as African Americans, as a people, have survived slavery, the

assumption is that we have been resilient to some extent. Therefore, select sources of Black psychology will be examined for
their interpretations of the *inner experience* of African Americans collectively for the purpose of constructing African American pastoral theology.

Traditional Psychology and African American Pastoral Theology

Although psychological theories based on a dominant culture can contribute to the construction of an African American
pastoral theology, we must acknowledge their inadequacies.
First, the same critique holds true for the developmental theories of traditional psychology as it does for traditional systematic theology: The determinism of traditional psychology has
not factored in the issues of race, gender, or class into its theories. Secondly, the emphasis on an individualistic approach limits the effectiveness for the critical psychological needs of the
African American community as a whole.

Traditional Psychology as Racially Oppressive

Traditional psychology has upheld the dominant cultural
ideology in its omission of race, gender, and class. Of course,
this is particularly problematic for poor African American
women. However, from Black women's (womanist) perspective, the collective experience of African Americans (men,
women, and children) has been negated in the conceptual
theories of traditional psychology. Racism is most pervasive.
Traditional theology's inherent racism is problematic for the
development of personality theory in the African American
context.

The fact that traditional psychology negates African American experience presupposes that the subjective experience of
African Americans has been deemed an insignificant factor to
consider in developmental theory. This is racial oppression—
consistent with White supremist ideology that considers Black
culture and experience to be inferior to the experience of White
dominant culture. The detriment of this approach and how it is
manifested is explained by African American pastoral psychologist Lee Butler, Jr.:

When hierarchial and dualistic ideologies are applied to culture, social status, or race, the African American tends to end up on the bottom rung or negative extreme.[1]

Thus, traditional psychology serves to impose the negative projections of White dominant culture on the psychology of African Americans as a racial and cultural group. In terms of personality development and identity formation, the other side of the projection is the introjection that is subject to occur as many African Americans either assimilate the views of the dominant White culture and/or internalize the distorted image of themselves. This becomes internalized oppression as African Americans accept the distortions as true and, in turn, begin to also negate their own culture and take on a kind of self-loathing as they view themselves as inferior to Whites. More will be said about internalized oppression in the course of this chapter. The point is that traditional psychology is racially oppressive, and the end result is that it has helped to create a negative psychical experience for African Americans in terms of our self-image. Therefore, the immediate challenge of Black psychology in terms of personality theory for African Americans is to address the omissions and to correct the distortions of traditional psychology.

The Individualistic Approach as Inadequate
Black psychologist Wade Nobles makes the point that a major difference in the cultural thought of African Americans and dominant culture is a retention of African philosophy that values the "experiential communality over individuality."[2] For example, as already mentioned in chapter 2, a communal concern of African Americans nationwide is the nihilism and despair that has seemingly engulfed the Black community of this country after nearly five centuries of sustained oppression (with no immediate end in sight). This is a psychological reality that

---

[1] Lee Butler, Jr., "Race, Religion, and African American Cultural Identity Formation" (Ph.D. diss., Drew University, 1994), 85.

[2] Wade W. Nobles, "African Philosophy: Foundations for Black Psychology," in *Black Psychology*, 3d ed., ed. Reginald L. Jones (Berkeley, Calif.: Cobb & Henry, 1991), 55.

threatens the very survival and liberation of African Americans, collectively. Therefore, it takes precedence over individual needs. That is not to say that there is not a concern for the individual in the African American context. On the contrary, for the African American context, the concern is to identify methodology that acknowledges and addresses the critical problems that African Americans face as individuals on a communal level. While the individualistic approach of traditional psychology has had a positive influence on the quality of one-on-one pastoral counseling in general, it does not offer much of a solution for the kinds of pastoral care interventions that are needed to address the most urgent psychological and spiritual needs of the masses of African Americans as a cultural group.

There are two additional factors that need consideration as we analyze the effectiveness of traditional psychology's individualistic approach for the African American context. First, it is common knowledge in the African American community that African Americans in large part have actively resisted individual therapy in traditional settings. This is due to a combination of the cultural preference that tends toward communality over individuality and/or an apparent lack of trust of White institutions historically, of which traditional psychology is one. Second, in light of the ecomonic data presented in chapter 2, it is reasonable to understand that the expense of individual therapy is beyond the means of the average African American family. As it is, clinical psychologist Nancy Boyd-Franklin acknowledges that the majority of poor African Americans involved in therapy are not self-referred, but usually referred (often under court order) by some societal agency that intrudes into their lives.[3] Therefore, overall, individualistic approaches for psychological intervention in the dominant cultural tradition have limited potential for accomplishing the task of bringing about the psychological healing needed in the African American community as a whole.

---

[3] For a discussion devoted to the subject of Blacks' resistance to clinical psychotherapy, see Nancy Boyd-Franklin, *Black Families in Therapy: A Multisystems Approach* (New York: Guilford Press, 1989), 158–75.

Black Psychology

What does the literature of Black psychology have to say about the experience of African Americans? Is there a schematic for addressing the existential problems of African Americans? Is there also a theme of survival and liberation in its vein?

The direction of Black psychology "has been heavily influenced by racism."[4] As already mentioned, when traditional psychology chooses to omit the cultural issues of race from its conceptual theories, that is racist. In that respect, Black psychology's response can be viewed as a kind of cultural psychology. However, Black psychology as a discipline is yet evolving. Aside from the fact that the conceptual framework for personality theories is beginning to emerge, Black psychology has not advanced to systematic kinds of approaches in ways similar to its cognate discipline, Black theology. Therefore, it is assumed that it will be some time before Black psychology can claim to have addressed the communal psychological issues of African Americans systematically. Currently, much Black psychological literature serves to argue against the deficiency approach to the Black experience prevalent in society's psychological and sociological literature, to give definition to Black psychology, and to argue for the distinctiveness of Black culture and functioning apart from the devaluative views of dominant European American culture.[5] One portion of the literature focuses on the value of African-centered thought as the conceptual basis for Black psychology. Another portion of the literature attempts to modify the modalities of traditional psychology to fit the African American context. And a significant portion of Black psychological literature serves to set forth therapeutic guidelines for intervention with the African American population.[6]

---

[4] Ibid., 162.

[5] In recent times, Black women such as Linda James Myers and Beverly Greene have also raised the issue of sexism in dominant culture and traditional psychology along with the concern of racism. See Linda James Myers, *Understanding an Afrocentric World View: Introduction to an Optimal Psychology* (Dubuque, Iowa: Kendal/Hunt 1988), 8–13; and Lillian Comas-Diaz and Beverly Greene, eds., *Women of Color: Integrating Ethnic and Gender Identities in Psychotherapy* (New York: Guilford Press, 1994).

[6] For examples see Joseph L. White, *The Psychology of Blacks* (Englewood Cliffs, N.J.: Prentice-Hall, 1984); Reginald L. Jones, ed., *Black Psychology*, 3d ed. (Berkeley, Calif.: Cobb & Henry, 1991); and Nancy Boyd-Franklin, *Black Families in Therapy: A Multisystems Approach* (New York: Guilford Press, 1989).

Although there is not a clear presence of Black liberation or womanist schools of thought per se, the themes of survival and liberation are implicit throughout the literature. Clearly the literature suggests that the objective of Black psychologists is to construct conceptual systems that will indeed help African Americans survive and to liberate the minds (consciously and unconsciously) of African Americans from the deep-level effects of their oppression. An underlying assumption of Black psychology is that African Americans will never be free or empowered to change our reality until our minds have been liberated not only from the lasting psychological effects of slavocracy but also from the negative psychological effects of Western psychology.[7]

Inasmuch as the literature of Black psychology comes together differently than the literature of Black theology, the approach of this chapter will be different. As opposed to focusing on the work of leading theorists in the field of Black psychology, a more cohesive approach will be to present topics in Black psychology that serve to interpret the African American experience and address the issues of survival and liberation in their own way. Three topical categories will be explored for that purpose: (1) Black psychology and the benefit of African-centered thought; (2) Black functioning and personality theories; and (3) Black clinical psychology and guidelines for intervention with African Americans.

Prior to an examination of the literature in the field of psychology, it will be helpful to set the stage for the psychological discussion with a brief historical overview of some of the psychological realities of African Americans that were existent during slavery. This is particularly significant because the institution of slavery has had a lasting effect on the collective psyche of African Americans, and it continues to influence the structures of contemporary American society. This will be discussed extensively throughout the chapter.

---

[7] Linda James Myers, *Understanding an Afrocentric World View: Introduction to an Optimal Psychology* (Dubuque, Iowa: Kendal/Hunt, 1988), 13.

A Psychological Snapshot of Slavery

In light of the dehumanizing treatment of Blacks physically and psychologically during slavery, it is quite logical to assume that much of the destructive behavior among African Americans described in chapter 2 (such as gang warfare, fratricide, etc.) is predictable—as a result of the lasting consequences of psychological abuse during slavery. It is, therefore, important to note that there was an intentionality on the part of White slave owners toward determining a lasting psychological enslavement of Blacks. This was also implied in chapter 2. However, in specific terms, evidence of the intent and purpose for the psychological enslavement of Blacks during slavery can be captured in the two following narratives:

> There are two ways in which a man [*sic*] can be enslaved: One is by force. He can be penned behind fences, guarded constantly, punished severely for breaking the slightest rule and made to live in constant fear…The second way was more subtle. Its aim was to brain wash the slave, to destroy his mind and replace it with the mind of the master. In that way the slave would enslave himself and there would be no need to police him. A slave should have no sense of himself that was separate from the self the master wanted him to have.[8]

> I have a fool-proof method for controlling your black slaves. I guarantee everyone of you that if installed correctly it will control the slaves for at least 300 years. My method is simple and members of your family or any overseer can use it…I have outlined a number of differences among the slaves; and I take these differences and make them bigger. I use fear, distrust, and envy for control purposes…you must pitch the old vs. the young black male, and the young against the old black male. You must use the dark skin slaves vs. the light skin slaves and the light skin slaves vs. the dark skin slaves. You must also have your white servants and overseers

---

[8] Julius Lester, *To Be A Slave* (New York: Scholastic, 1968), 76.

distrust all blacks, but it is necessary that your slaves trust and depend on us. They must love, respect and trust only us.[9]

These narratives—one representing a slave and the other representing a slave master—illustrate that implicit in the motivation to enslave the minds of Blacks was an economic concern to secure and prolong the institution of slavery. Yet it was the audaciousness of White supremacy that accompanied slavocracy that assumed the right to employ tactics to brainwash and control the thinking of Black slaves. The intent of the psychological abuse was to ensure that the behavior of Blacks would be predictable, to undermine the slaves' sense of identity and security in unity that Blacks held among themselves so that Blacks would remain under the control of Whites for years to come by their own internalized oppression (even in the absence of physical abuse). Hence, slaves were coerced into accepting their inferior status to Whites in every respect and were taught to distrust, disrespect, even hate, themselves and one another.

To the extent that these tactics of psychological abuse took hold in the Black psyche, this aspect of the psychological legacy of African Americans is not the basis for a very healthy psychological picture of African Americans. Fortunately, in recent years Black psychologists have stepped up to the task of researching and interpreting another side of the psychological picture of African Americans: the legacy of Africans who arrived in the New World and were able to hold to and sustain in themselves and their descendants a very healthy philosophical understanding of God, themselves, and the world around them. The following section presents selected sources in Black psychology that acknowledge the reality of this legacy.

Black Psychology and African-Centered Thought

Although the approach of some Black psychologists since the early 1970s has been to find their theoretical home in the

---

[9] The "Willie Lynch Speech" (dated 1712), delivered by Willie Lynch (an invited speaker and plantation owner in the West Indies) to plantation owners in the Colony of Virginia.

appropriation of traditional concepts of Western psychology,[10] leading Black psychologist Wade Nobles has built a case for grounding Black psychology in African philosophy. Nobles' assertion is that the sum of Black psychology is something more than the experience of "having been forced into dehumanizing conditions." Nobles' research produces convincing evidence that Black history of preslavery times continues to have significant bearing on the psychology of African Americans in the present as well as our most recent past. There is, in fact, evidence of the retention of African philosophy in the behavior of Black people throughout their duration in America.[11] Therefore, he states:

> [T]he task of black psychology is to offer an understanding of the behavioral definition of African philosophy and to document what, if any, modifications it has undergone during particular experiential periods.[12]

Nobles' assertion is that the basis of African philosophy is observable in the religious behavior of Africans—that philosophy and religion are the same phenomenon in African culture. Behaviorally there are "two prevailing aspects of the African ethos" that have survived and can be observed in the religious and psychological phenomenon of African Americans from preslavery in Africa, throughout slavery, and into contemporary times: (1) a philosophy of "survival of the people"; and (2) a "oneness with nature." Accordingly, these two aspects—consistent with the African adage "I am because we are. And, because we are, therefore, I am"—are the focal

---

[10] For example, the early works of noted Black psychologists such as Na'im Akbar and Adlebert H. Jenkins evolved around the humanistic approach of traditional psychology. See Na'im Akbar, "The Evolution of Human Psychology for African Americans," in Reginald L. Jones, ed., *Black Psychology*, 3d ed.(Berkeley, Calif.: Cobb & Henry, 1991), 99–121, and Adlebert H. Jenkins, "A Humanistic Approach to Black Psychology," in Reginald L. Jones, ed., *Black Psychology*, 3d ed. (Berkeley, Calif.: Cobb & Henry, 1991), 79–97. Notably, although Akbar had reservations about theories founded in African philosophy, his work increasingly over the years has advanced the idea of African philosophy as foundational to Black psychology; his latest book is *Light from Ancient Africa* (Tallahassee, Fla.: Mind Productions & Associates, 1994).

[11] Nobles, 47–63.

[12] Ibid., 62.

points that foster an understanding of Black psychology over time.[13]

Nobles' interpretation of African American experience says (contrary to the popular assumption) that the dehumanizing experience of slavery was not enough to totally erase the collective memory of African ethos. His implication is that, in spite of the fact that "divide and conquer" tactics and other forms of psychological oppression and repression were used (and continue to be used) against African Americans, the notion of "we" as a Black people (regardless of tribe, hue, shape, or size) has survived. This notion translates into an identity that is Black.[14]

Notably, Nobles also argues that very often it was the oppression itself that enabled the retention of African philosophy and culture. Specifically, the isolation and segregation were integral parts of the oppression that served to foster and reinforce the African way of life in an alien culture. And, quite naturally, another factor that aided the retention of African culture was that some of African culture did not conflict with the alien culture of the of the slave masters. For example, despite the fact that Africans were not permitted to read or write, African oral tradition served to sustain survival knowledge down through the generations. In actuality, what occurred in the private and public lives of Blacks was a masterful interaction between African philosophy and Western philosophy. Hence, Nobles also refers to African Americans as "americanized Africans."[15]

Although Black psychologist (and accomplished musician) Arthur C. Jones acknowledges that his book *Wade in the Water: The Wisdom of the Spirituals*[16] was conceived in a "serendipitous" manner, its approach is very much in line with Nobles' mandate for Black psychology as stated above. In fact, Jones's book serves to illustrate how African philosophy manifested in the behavior of African Americans during the period of slavery. Jones's research on the musical genre known as spirituals, which was created by slaves, offers a great deal of insight into the

---

[13] Ibid., 49–56.

[14] Ibid., 56–60.

[15] Ibid., 57–63.

[16] Arthur C. Jones, *Wade in the Water: The Wisdom of the Spirituals* (New York: Orbis Books, 1993).

behavior of Africans and how the institution of slavery modified that behavior. Following is Jones's personal testimony of his journey toward gaining an understanding of the significance of the spirituals for psychology as his book began to take form:

> As I found myself almost singlemindedly focused on the spirituals...my emerging conviction [was] that the music early African Americans created is archetypally relevant to the human experience, extending beyond the folk community of origin...But my experience of researching and performing African American spirituals helped deepen my understanding of African American psychology in ways I could not have imagined. I began to understand much more fully that the spiritual songs that originated in slavery are important and accessible survivals of culture that had within it elements of extraordinary healing power. I also began to understand that the spirituals reflect a central core of African American culture, upon whose foundations almost all other aspects of our psychological and social history have been built.[17]

Jones's reflections are an acknowledgment that the spirituals provide clear evidence of African culture that has survived in African American culture. Not only were they "survivals of culture," but Jones's research reveals that the spirituals served to transmit the wisdom of African philosophy into the slave culture that had everything to do with the slaves' "survival" in the alien culture. Inasmuch as the slave culture required that slaves repress their knowledge of themselves as free Africans, their primary strategy for survival of the people was to find ways to sustain that awareness, spiritually and psychologically, without the knowledge of their masters. Thus, the spirituals—a modification of the oral tradition—came to be a significant medium through which coded messages were communicated between the Africans. Psychic and spiritual healing power came through the songs and dance of the spiritual music—offsetting the psychological damage intended by the oppression. In this

---

[17] Ibid., xiii–xiv.

respect, the spirituals provided a strong psychological foundation for the survival of Africans as a people in America.[18]

In a general sense, Jones asserts that there are universal
lessons in the music of the spirituals from which modern
psychology can benefit.[19] In terms of the African American
context, spirituals serve to communicate "a great deal of wisdom
and guidance concerning personal and social issues" past and
present. Yet Jones argues that a major hindrance to our understanding the value of the spirituals—whether we are Black or
White—results from the "racism that permeates American society." That is, we have had a tendency to overlook their value
because we tend to devalue African American culture.[20]

Molefi Kete Asante is a professor of African American studies. Much of his research and study have been concerned with
the psychology of African people. Primarily, Asante asserts an
ideology of afrocentrism, which promotes the psychological
value of placing African philosophy and African cultural heritage at the center of the lives of African people. Because most
African people of the world have been colonized and domi-
nated by their oppressors, Asante's concern has been for African descendants to recover their repressed cultural heritage.
Asante argues that the letting go of the African way of life has
been most detrimental to the psychological well-being of African Americans and our ability to take control of our lives.[21]

The psychology of the African without Afrocentricity has
become a matter of great concern. Instead of looking out from
one's own center, the non-Afrocentric person operates in a manner that is predictably negative. The person's images, symbols,
lifestyles, and manners are contradictory and thereby destructive to personal and collective growth and development.[22]

---

[18] Ibid., 10–11.
[19] Jones is referring to Carl Jung's concept of universal archetypes and how
the images and symbolism of the spirituals may offer meaning not only to African
Americans, but universally to all of humanity. Jones finds this concept attractive
and useful, along with contemporary Jungians, despite Carl Jung's otherwise negative racial thinking. His commentary can be found in the notes of his book *Wade in
the Water*, 161–62.
[20] Ibid., 13.
[21] Molefi Kete Asante, *Afrocentricity*, rev. ed. (Trenton, N.J.: Africa World
Press, 1988).
[22] Ibid., 1.

On the basis of Asante's research of African history and culture, his ideology of Afrocentricity can be viewed as a kind of self-help psychology for Blacks. Asante's logic is that the most basic need of African people who have inhabited and been forced to adapt and assimilate an alien culture is to recover their African beginnings and way of life. Therefore, the purpose of Asante's ideology serves to raise African-centered thought and the possibility of its transformative benefits to the conscious awareness of African Americans (and others of African descent who have been colonized).

Asante argues that the more African Americans move in the direction of claiming and affirming an identification with Africa on the personal and collective level, the healthier we will be psychologically and the more in control we will be of our lives, individually and as a people. Interestingly, Asante also claims that there is evidence of the retention of African philosophy and sensibilities in the collective psyche of African Americans. However, it is more of a collective unconsciousness that has begun to "invade" African American behavior. For example, in terms of the ongoing struggle for survival, oneness, and unity among the African diaspora residing in America, it is our unconscious remembrance of ourselves as free Africans that has moved us to claim "consciously" our collective identity. In doing so, we have collectively rejected the names "negroes" or "coloreds," given to us by Whites, and instead named ourselves as "Africans," "Blacks," "Afro-Americans," and most recently "African Americans." Asante believes that once individuals awaken to the African knowledge of themselves, they will act in a conscious way to take control over their lives; a first indication of this will be when individuals begin to choose African names for themselves and their family members.[23]

---

[23]At the time of Asante's initial writing of *Afrocentricity* the term *Afro-American* was widely accepted among Blacks in America, and it served to accommodate his use of the term *Afrocentricity* nicely. However, about the time his revised edition was published, the term *African American* was beginning to take hold in the consciousness of African descendants in America. The term *African American* acknowledges the need for African descendants in American to reconcile the sense of "twoness" (African, yet American) that we feel as described by W. E. B. Dubois in his book *The Souls of Black Folk*. The term *Afro-American* is seldom used anymore because, while it does imply African ancestry, the term *African American* more accurately captures the intent to describe people who are both African and American.

Presenting her perspective as an African American woman, psychologist Linda James Myers raises the fact that African American women have to deal with psychological oppression in terms of gender and class as well as racism, and that Western society in general has negative psychological effects. Building on her research of African philosophy and culture, Myers' intent in her book *Understanding an Afrocentric World View: Introduction to an Optimal Psychology* presents more than an ideology. It is an introduction to an Afrocentric paradigm that addresses the specific psychological needs of African Americans, but also that serves as a corrective to traditional Western psychology in general.[24]

Myers' assertion is that the limited reasoning of traditional psychology is suboptimal for all of humanity in general and for African Americans in particular. In general, the "segmented" way of thinking—thinking that is hierarchial, individualistic, dichotomous, dualistic, and so forth—that is foundational to Western psychology creates and fosters harmful psychological functioning in general. This partially explains why and how racial oppression is so prevalent in America: Racism is the result of negative psychological functioning (such as inner feelings of "inadequacy, anxiety, guilt, resentment, and hostility") that builds up in racial attitudes (of those who, in their hierarchial and dualistic thinking, believe in White supremacy) and are projected onto Blacks.[25] In this respect, Myers claims that traditional psychology has been a "psychology of oppression" for African Americans in particular:

> We have as a people experienced the psychology of oppression, and it is the sub-optimal worldview that is oppressive. We have been lead to believe that our very physical survival was in the hands of another man; we have been denied access to the truth about our cultural heritage and history; our cultural heritage and history have been negated and that of sub-optimal thinkers elevated.[26]

---

[24] Linda James Myers, *Understanding an Afrocentric World View: Introduction to an Optimal Psychology* (Dubuque, Iowa: Kendall/Hunt, 1988).

[25] Ibid., 14.

[26] Ibid., 15.

Therefore, there is a specific charge to Black psychologists amid Myers' inclusive approach to all of the field of psychology: If African Americans are to survive and be liberated from psychological oppression and, therefore, be in control of our choices and the direction of our lives, Black psychology must develop "methods for the structuring of consciousness" in such a way that African Americans are directed to the true history of ourselves and the knowledge of an Afrocentric worldview. Myers argues that the psychology of an Afrocentric worldview is optimal for African Americans because its philosophical undergirdings—which are spiritual, communal, multidimensional, diunital, and so on—point the way to needed transformation and psychic healing.[27]

Black Psychology and Personality Theory

The subject of African American personality is quite challenging to Black psychology as a field. Its issues are multifaceted and quite complex. Yet there is an urgent need to come to terms with the complexity if African Americans are to be free from the psychological burdens of our oppressive culture, past and present, and self-determine our lives. Black psychologist Kobi Kambon (formerly Joseph A. Baldwin) asserts that traditional Western psychology's conceptions of personality theory are responsible in part for the psychological oppression that African Americans continue to experience in contemporary times. The primary reason that traditional theories of psychology are oppressive for African Americans is because conceptually they view African Americans as "determined" by a Eurocentric worldview. This determination begins with the history of African enslavement in America, assumes genetic inferiority, and makes unilateral assumptions about the African American experience in light of the European American experience.[28]

African American pastoral psychologist Lee Butler, Jr., agrees that the determinism of traditional Western psychology has been detrimental and inadequate for the African American

---

[27] Ibid., 11–15.
[28] Kobi Kazembe Kalongi Kambon, *The African Personality in America* (Tallahassee, Fla.: NUBIAN Nation Publications, 1992), 31–33.

context.[29] However, his approach to Black psychology (ultimately, African American pastoral psychology) in his doctoral dissertation illustrates one attempt to modify traditional psychological theory to fit the African American context.[30]

Basically, Butler's approach to the psychological methodology grounds Jung's analytical psychology in Erikson's theory of identity formation. For the African American context, Butler's attraction to Jung has to do with Jung's attention to genetics and the concept of human collectivity (including "functions of the collective unconscious") as it relates to identity, history, symbolism, culture, and religion. Erikson's emphasis on early childhood development, identity formation, and the self discussed in terms of "the individuals in social and relational experiences" is attractive because it is compatible with the communal issues of African Americans.[31]

Although Butler is able to find the basis for appropriating a traditional psychodynamic methodology to the African American context through Erikson's approach, he also acknowledges the limitations. In addition to the fact that Erikson (like his predecessors, Freud and Jung) does not consider the "historical and psychological oppression of African Americans,"[32] Butler argues that there are other serious limitations in Erikson's theory for the African American context: (1) Its "understandings of humanity are dualistic." (2) Although it acknowledges "hope" as an activity of development, it does not "articulate the essence of hope." (3) It implies that a "false identity," as the "first identity" that is developed, is the lasting identity. In short, adoption and assimilation of Erikson's theory by itself serves to foster a "false identity" for most African Americans; they would tend to function in a state of always renegotiating their inner conflicts in order to try to accommodate Erikson's positive and preferable pole in dominant society.[33]

---

[29] Lee Butler, Jr., "Race, Religion, and African American Cultural Identity Formation: An Erickson Approach" (Ph.D. diss., Drew University, 1994), 85.

[30] Butler's dissertation in its entirety employs a phenomenological method that he calls "Psycho-theology." The term denotes an approach that is also an integration of psychology and theology. However, Butler combines Eriksonian psychology and systematic theologies, including Black theology.

[31] Ibid., 8–9, 168.

[32] Ibid., 173.

[33] Ibid., 119–22.

Moving beyond Erikson's human stage development, Butler presents a corrective approach, "The Dichotomy of Issues." Butler explains that his intent is not to imitate the dualism in Erikson's model, but to acknowledge the "dichotomous, dialectic legacy" of the African American identity.

> The African American identity is the resulting compilation of African retentions, appropriations, and accommodation within the United States of America's social structure.[34]

Butler's Dichotomy of Issues also asserts that, universally, there are different issues of identity formation to be considered during the "foundational" and "constructive" periods of life.[35] However, the significance is vital to the African American context because all of the issues of each developmental period need to be accounted for and adequately addressed. Butler explains the logic of the African American cultural perspective:

> The Dichotomy of Issues says that there are particular issues that the developing individual will confront during formative years of life, and that a variation of those same issues are confronted throughout the course of adulthood. This means that the issues and formative experiences of childhood are the "blueprints" for interpreting and constructing adulthood...The Dichotomy of Issues suggests that the African American psyche, which moves according to its roots in African spirituality, makes accommodations according to the circumstances of a given moment. It does not respond to the expectations of the context, nor the stage of description, but according to the psyche's understanding of the issues and self-concept. If the expectations of the context were always in charge, the African would never have become an African American.[36]

The Dichotomy of Issues considerably reduces the idea of determinism by a Eurocentric worldview for African Americans.

---

[34] Ibid., 180.
[35] Ibid., 179–182.
[36] Ibid., 177–78.

It clarifies that aside from early life formations, African Americans have a core identity that remains from our African cultural heritage, and that is negotiated and renegotiated in light of the issues that life presents within American society.

Aligned with Erikson's model, Butler's construct on the foundational side of issues is the *historical self*, which pertains to the emergence of the individual African American self. On the constructive side of issues, *spirituality* is the construct that refers to the emergence of the communal self. The issues of the *historical self* and *spirituality* are unconscious guides. A third construct, *rage/creativity* is the line between the *historical self* and *spirituality* representing the destructive or constructive responses of African Americans to our American environment. In light of the oppressive realities of American life, in particular, African Americans are challenged to creatively develop coping skills to offset the internal sense of rage[37] that often accompanies the awareness of society's injustices.[38]

While Butler's approach appears to address the multiplicity of issues in the development of individual/communal identity formation in African Americans, Kobi Kambon considers this kind of approach as flawed. His assertion is that methodology that modifies a Eurocentric worldview continues to subject the African American experience to that worldview. The result is still cultural domination rather than cultural relativism.[39]

---

[37] Black psychiatrists Price M. Cobbs and William H. Grier wrote a book titled *Black Rage*. Their intent is to explain the phenomenon of Black rage (an effect of slavery and institutionalized racism in this country) on the psyche of Black Americans. With this explanation also comes an explanation of what Black rage is for all of American society to be mindful of. The authors want American society to understand that, after generations of senseless and cruel oppression, each and every Black has a sense of growing rage within them, which is justifiable considering the injustices that have been done and continue to be done to Black people in this country. The primary message of the book puts all on notice: that Black rage is a problem that this country needs to be aware of particularly because it is not just a reality for some angry revolutionaries who might be seen marching, demonstrating, or uprising in the news media, or persons incarcerated for violent crimes. The multitude of African Americans have very real feelings of rage inside themselves; this is regardless of whether it is visible or not, conscious or unconscious. The rage is there under the surface. Further, Black rage is not just a Black problem. White society must take responsibility for its existence and work through the problem with Blacks. See William Grier and Price Cobb, *Black Rage* (New York: Basic Books, 1968).

[38] Ibid., 180–83.

[39] Kambon, 20.

The thesis of Kambon's book *The African Personality in America: An African-Centered Framework* is that the African personality, though it is sometimes disguised, distorted, and often manifested unconsciously, is most determined by an Afrocentric worldview. The phenomenon of its ontological features of kinship and community, relations and life, religion and symbolisms of the African Americans can be observed in the behavior of African Americans and the African diaspora throughout the world. Specifically, African American psychical reality as expressed through our "music, songs, our vibrant and deeply-felt emotionality, our religious fervor, and our fundamental moral temperament" points to the African source of our personality.[40]

In short, Kambon asserts that the phenomenon of the African personality is distinct. His basic assumptions are that evidence of this phenomenon observed in the collective expressions of African people, regardless of their social location, is a result of biogenetics and intrapsychic phenomenon more than social and environmental influences. Quite naturally, when these assumptions are applied to the African personality, three premises evolve:

> (1) [T]hat African personality is "African," racially and culturally speaking, in its basic nature; (2) that the exposure of African personality to European culture and the White-supremacy forces of racial-cultural oppression have only substantially affected its conscious expressive dimension and not its basic African nature as well; and (3) that "Africanity," in the sense of Cosmology/worldview, dominates the personality pattern of racially-mixed individuals of part African descent if its biogenetic presence (African genetic structure) is minimally evident in the phenotype/physiological characteristics of the person.[41]

Addressing, primarily, the predicament of African Americans—many of whom are "racially mixed"—Kambon goes on to say:

---

[40] Ibid., 15.
[41] Ibid., 41.

This last premise addresses the biogenetic predicament of particularly Africans in the American hemisphere, where the brutal raping of African women and men occurred for over three centuries, producing the phenomenon of miscegenation/ "mulattonization" of substantial numbers of the African race.[42]

Building on Kambon's comment, it should stand to reason that identification with "Africanity" on the part of racially mixed African Americans has also been influenced by the racism in American society. That is, the evidence of African biogenetics in their physical appearance is the basis for racial rejection in dominant society, serving to reinforce conscious embracing and nurture of the African personality by racially mixed African Americans.

Hence, Kambon insists that it is imperative that Black psychology give due consideration to the above assumptions and premises for the conceptual framework in the construction of paradigms for African American personality theory. Further, Kambon asserts specific criteria that is fundamental to the development of a "functionally relevant model of the African personality":

The first fundamental requirement for a truly relevant model of African personality is that the model must be "Africentric" ideologically and philosophically…The second requirement is that the model must include a biogenetic influence or determinant in the African personality formula…[T]hirdly, a functionally relevant model must explain the basic "African nature" of the African psyche, apart from European cultural oppression and assimilation affects on the African personality…The fourth basic requirement is that the model must explain how European cultural oppression/White supremacy domination has affected African personality functioning…The fifth requirement is that the model must explain, or suggest, how to maintain "order" or normal functioning in African personality and how to restore order where disorder occurs…The sixth and final

[42] Ibid.

requirement for a truly functionally relevant model of African personality is that it should have explicit liberation implications or consequences for the African mind.[43]

In closing this discussion on Black psychology and the development of African American personality theory, it is important to note that each of the discussants argue against the determinism of traditional Western psychology for a developmental theory of African Americans. Their intent is to construct paradigms that serve to eliminate the oppressive determinism of a Eurocentric worldview in traditional psychology's conceptual framework and to correct the negative effects on the African American psyche from slavery and racist structures that continue to exist in American society. Butler is willing to attempt to modify traditional psychology. Yet the flaw that Kambon speaks of is evident as Butler names his modified version a *Dichotomy of Issues*. Therefore, Butler's model serves more as a bridge to traditional psychology than a corrective. Kambon's approach is purely phenomenological, stressing that preslavery history and/or an Afrocentric worldview are positively deterministic in the formation of the African American personality.

Clinical Intervention with African Americans

Up to this point the discussion has been focused primarily on the psychical experience of African people and their descendants as a result of slavery and racial oppression in a general sense. In the process, we have only begun to skim the surface of the inner experience of African Americans in contemporary times. However, the nature of the relationship between therapist and client, which has potential for developing trust and a certain amount of intimacy, provides an invaluable resource to the rest of the field for insight into psychical experience of African Americans today.

In light of the yet-developing nature of Black psychology, as the field continues to sort through the multifaceted issues of Black culture in America, Black clinical psychologists have not

---

[43] Ibid., 45–47.

had the benefit of crystallized theories of personality development to draw on. Nancy Boyd-Franklin explains that, for the
most part, Black clinicians draw on their knowledge of African
legacy, the impact of slavery, racism, discrimination, and the
contemporary American society's victim system in their work
with African American clients. [44]

Highlighting the fact that much of the mental energy that
African Americans expend has to do with their need and ability to adapt to the external influences of society, Arthur Jones
created a conceptual model for clinical use. He graphically illustrates four overlapping circles out of which an arrow points
to a fifth circle. The four circles represent four classes of interre-
lated variables that African Americans must respond to in their
daily living: (1) reactions to racial oppression; (2) influence of
the majority culture; (3) influence of Afro-American culture; and
(4) personal endowments. The fifth circle, to which an arrow
points from the cluster of circles, represents the presenting problem for therapy that may be influenced by any of the four variables unique to African American existence in this country, or
all of the four variables as they interact with each other.[45]

In terms of adult development that is specific to African
Americans, strategies of adaptation to the oppressive racial
climate of America are necessary for healthy psychological
functioning. Jones's discussion around clinical cases in which
racism was a presenting issue reveals that racial oppression in
contemporary American society manifests in more subtle ways.
Consistent with what has already been discussed by other Black
psychologists in this book (about the reasoning and nature behind racism in this country), Jones is quite clear that by the time
African Americans reach adulthood, if not sooner, we need to
have developed mental strategies of adjustment to offset the
negative projections of majority White society onto African

---

[44] Boyd-Franklin, *Black Families in Therapy*, 7–12. The "victim system" is the
way structures of contemporary society impose real barriers to African American
achievement. More will be said about it later in the discussion.

[45] Arthur C. Jones, "Psychological Functioning in African-American Adults:
Some Elaborations on a Model, With Clinical Applications," in *Black Adult
Development and Aging*, ed. Reginald L. Jones (Berkeley, Calif.: Cobb & Henry, 1989),
297–307.

Americans as a cultural group. The point is made for clinical application with African American clients that, although the form of racial oppression may manifest differently for African American men than for African American women (requiring different adaptive strategies), all African Americans are subjected to racial oppression—"regardless of social class or geographical location."

Specific to the dynamics of the inner psychical experience of African Americans, Jones's case material suggests that when racial oppression is recognized, emotions within African Americans (unconscious and conscious) range anywhere from feelings of rage and anger to feelings of vulnerability and panic. And, as intended by the racial oppression in the first place, general feelings of disempowerment, insecurity, and self-doubt are likely to be experienced in the inner selves of African Americans unless coping or adjustment skills are developed.[46]

Racism is so prevalent in American society today that it is difficult to separate its influence from the other variables that are unique to the African American experience. Turning to Jones's second variable—"the influences of majority culture"—the connection with racism is easily made. According to Jones, depending on how great the desire of an individual African American is to interface with or assimilate dominant culture, the greater the sense of rejection when it comes. Inevitably, situations will arise when African Americans are not welcomed, or even allowed, to participate in areas of the mainstream of society that Whites take for granted. As a result, the negative reaction of many African Americans is to internalize the rejection and experience "self-alienation." Others, according to Jones, employ the dangerous defense mechanism of denial in face of these realities. Jones's suggestions to clinicians working with African Americans is to aid the development of the ability to separate from the negative influences of the majority, and to make decisions that do not compromise personal integrity.[47]

In essence, Jones agrees with other Black psychologists that, in the face of racial oppression, there is tremendous mental

---

[46] Ibid., 298–301.
[47] Ibid., 301–3.

health benefit to African Americans who are able to embrace the "influences of traditional African-American culture." Once African Americans are able to reconnect and identify with the *core* of themselves as African descendants with a rich cultural heritage, there is basis to anchor/reanchor an inner balance.[48]

Finally, Jones's discussion about "personal experience and endowments" and how they influence development in African Americans cautions therapists not to overlook the importance of these influences while focusing on racial oppression or cultural factors. That is to say, rather than going to the other extreme of focusing primarily on racial and cultural issues, at the expense of the personal issues, a balance needs to be maintained that keeps all four of the variables in perspective. Personal experience and endowments are significant because they serve to give information regarding an individual's strengths and weaknesses.[49]

Nancy Boyd-Franklin's book *Black Families in Therapy: A Multisystems Approach* serves to enlarge Jones's discussion in that she highlights issues related to the uniqueness of African American family structure and considers the specific issues of poor African Americans as well as middle-class African Americans. Boyd-Franklin also provides guidelines for clinical intervention. Basically, the book introduces a multisystems approach with extensive illustrations of case material and suggestions for clinical application, which addresses the cultural issues of African American individuals and their families.[50]

In addition to Boyd-Franklin's discussion on her multisystems approach in clinical interventions with Black families, her book serves to fill a void in the literature on Black psychology. There are thorough descriptions of the preslavery legacy of African Americans, the impact of slavery, and racial oppression and discrimination in the structures of contemporary American society as well as their negative psychological effects on African Americans. Inasmuch as the majority of the

---

[48] Ibid., 303–04.

[49] Ibid., 304–06.

[50] Nancy Boyd-Franklin, *Black Families in Therapy: A Multisystems Approach* (New York: Guilford Press, 1989).

discussion in this chapter so far has focused on the slavery and preslavery experience, for the purpose of the discussion in this section, the emphasis of Boyd-Franklin's discussion will focus on the contemporary experience of African Americans.

Building on Jones's discussion of racial oppression and the influence of majority culture, Boyd-Franklin introduces the concept of the *victim system* and the experience of African American poor into the discussion. The sociological data presented on the status of African Americans in chapter 2 indicates that African Americans, in numbers disproportionate to their White counterparts, are undereducated, unemployed, underemployed, and so on. In the face of what can become genocidal poverty, the hope of poor African Americans in particular (and many African Americans in general) is that they will somehow be able to acquire an economic material base through education, employment, ownership, and so forth. Yet Boyd-Franklin acknowledges that the futility of the efforts of many African Americans to rise above their dire circumstances causes them to feel and believe that they are *victimized* by the influences of the majority society. To support her argument that a victim system exists in this country, not only in the minds of many African Americans, but in the structures of American society, Boyd-Franklin documents the observations of social worker Elaine Pinderhughes:

> A victim system is a circular feedback process that exhibits properties such as stability, predictability and identity that are common to all systems. This particular system threatens self-esteem and reinforces problematic responses in communities, families and individuals. The feedback works as follows: Barriers to opportunity and education limit the chance for achievement, employment, and the attainment of skill. This limitation can, in turn, lead to poverty or stress in relationships, which interferes with adequate performance of family roles. Strains in family roles cause problems in individual growth and development and limit the opportunities of families to meet their own needs or to

organize to improve their communities. Communities limited in resources (jobs, education, housing, etc.) are unable to support families properly and the community all too often becomes itself an active disorganizing influence, a breeder of crime and other pathology, and a cause of even more powerlessness.[51]

Boyd-Franklin's concern is that clinicians who work with African Americans need to be aware of the feelings of victimization, low self-esteem, and hopelessness that African Americans experience as a result of their current experience of racial oppression. Boyd-Franklin also wants clinicians to understand the unique kind of victimization that African Americans have experienced and continue to experience on the basis of the color of our skin—African Americans are the only racial group that has experienced forced immigration to this country as slaves.

The importance of bringing the issues of African American families to the forefront of clinical therapy has to do with how Black family dynamics have been negatively stereotyped and labeled as dysfunctional in majority society. Clinicians need to understand that much of the attack on the Black family in the literature has been based on a stereotypical view of African American women as matriarchs who dominate and emasculate Black men, and of extended family structures viewed as deficient.[52] Boyd-Franklin's intent, therefore, is to counter society's negative myths surrounding the African American family and to present a truer picture of African American family dynamics and the strength of extended family structures.[53]

In addition to whatever therapeutic changes that are needed for respective African American families, Boyd-Franklin's overall goal in treatment is empowerment. Psychological empowerment of African Americans will enable us to confront the demeaning and harmful psychological effects of racism and

---

[51] Elaine Pinderhughes in Boyd-Franklin, 11.

[52] This view was widely adopted and appropriated in sociological and psychological literature, as well as public opinion, following the release and publication of a governmental report written by Patrick D. Moynihan on the Black family. See Patrick D. Moynihan, *The Negro Family: The Case for National Action* (Washington, D.C.: U.S. Department of Labor, 1965).

[53] Boyd-Franklin, 14–17.

victimization. Boyd-Franklin points out that, in particular, role flexibility and the principle of reciprocity (helping each other out) that exist in Black families are central in family relations and important "survival mechanisms" of the community. Therefore, key to the achievement of empowerment (through therapy) is the therapist's affirmation of the strengths of the extended family structure and kinship networks that are integral to African American culture. Black families, on the other hand, need to reclaim and embrace the evidence of their African heritage that exemplifies the philosophy of unity and communal concern in their family structure and dynamics.[54]

A multisystems approach, according to Boyd-Franklin, requires that therapists prepare themselves to work with all the various issues and levels of Black family dynamics and interactions with the surrounding community:

> [E]ffective therapy with Black families requires from the therapist a flexibility that allows her or him to draw from different systems theories and incorporate them into an overall treatment plan. It also requires that we be prepared to intervene at a variety of system levels, such as individual, family, extended family, church, community, and social services.[55]

Working with poor Black families, for example, may involve many different levels and systems. The therapist must not only have knowledge of the African American culture and all the many levels of its systems and structures (from single-parent families to nuclear families, extended families, and kinship networks, to the Black church, etc.). But the therapist must also have knowledge of various societal structures such as schools, social service agencies, community organizations, and so on, in order to help the families navigate these systems.[56] Clearly, the necessary preparation for a multisystems approach is extensive when one considers the necessary training and theoretical knowledge that is required, as well as the work clinicians should involve themselves in to know themselves.

---

[54] Ibid., 15–16.
[55] Ibid., 133–34.
[56] Ibid., 158.

Specifically, Boyd-Franklin's multisystems approach is a combination of three theoretic approaches to family therapy. First, structural family therapy is integrated for its usefulness in family problem solving.[57] The second approach, the Bowenian model of therapy, provides insight and strategies for working with extended families, and includes the benefit of a multigenerational approach to family therapy.[58] The third theory, named "Paradox/Strategy/Systemic Approaches," provides resources for working with resistance and power struggles in family therapy.[59] It is Boyd-Franklin's contention that in light of the Black family's needs, the integration of these three models for family therapy, along with preparation of one's self as a tool for therapy, is a strong basis for successful intervention with Black families. However, she insists that any therapist can come up with other kinds of multisystems approaches that may work equally as well as this one.[60]

According to Boyd-Franklin, most important in working with Black families is the process of "joining" with the family. If a therapist has not taken time to prepare him or herself for what is required to be able to join with a family in therapeutic relations, the initial encounter may fail. Therefore, definite groundwork has to be laid before a therapist has the foundation necessary to be able to initiate and engage in a therapeutic relationship with African Americans.[61] Following are guidelines that will benefit the therapeutic process with Black families, which are noteworthy guidelines for pastoral counseling with African American families or pastoral care relations with African Americans in general.

First, all therapists (or pastoral caregivers) need to be able to understand the insidiousness of racism. White therapists need to be able to confront racism within themselves. Black

---

[57] See S. Minuchin, *Families and Family Therapy* (Cambridge, Mass.: Harvard University Press, 1974), and S. Minuchin and C. Fishman, eds. *Family Therapy Techniques* (Cambridge, Mass.: Harvard Universtity Press, 1981).

[58] See Murray Bowen, *Family Therapy in Clinical Practice* (New York: Jason Aronson, 1978).

[59] See P. Papp, "Paradoxes," in *Family Therapy Techniques,* ed. S. Minuchin and C. Fishman (Cambridge, Mass.: Harvard University Press, 1981).

[60] Boyd-Franklin, 131.

[61] Ibid., 95.

therapists will have to avoid the trap of over-identification with racial issues. This is particularly important as it pertains to issues of transference, counter-transference, and the therapist's ability to join with the family. Boyd-Franklin stresses that the issue of trust is a particularly sensitive issue for African Americans:

> Black people, because of the often extremely subtle ways in which racism manifests itself socially, are particularly attuned to very fine distinctions among such variables in all interactions—with other Blacks, with White people, and with White institutions. Because of this, many Black people have been socialized to pay attention to the nuances of behavior and not just the verbal message.[62]

Second, successful therapeutic relations with Black families require that the therapist has the ability to use one's self in therapy. This will entail being very aware of one's own culture, the dynamics of one's own family of origin, and the issues that may arise as a result of these awarenesses. Important questions that Boyd-Franklin suggests each therapist ask her- or himself, regardless of their race are: Which parts of my "family culture" have I accepted and rejected? and Why do I want to work with Black families? These kinds of questions cause one to confront one's own issues and motivations. The implication is that having "missionary tendencies" or other unresolved family issues that could be projected onto the family in therapy would be detrimental to the therapeutic relationship.[63]

Third, a strong therapeutic alliance with Black families entails having the ability to negotiate values and beliefs. There are a range of issues that may come up in therapy that center on the questions of one's values and beliefs. Depending on the nature of the issues, the opinions that are subject to be expressed may be strongly felt. Some of the issues may pertain to race and discrimination, views on abortion, religious beliefs, and so forth. Regardless of the therapist's own system of beliefs and values, it is imperative that the therapist avoid imposing her or his

---

[62] Ibid., 96.
[63] Ibid., 99.

beliefs in the course of therapy. On the contrary, it would be beneficial for the therapist to have some previous knowledge about distinctive values and beliefs that are central to African American culture, such as extended family dynamics and the high regard for spirituality and religious beliefs in African American culture.[64]

Conclusion

Given this discussion carried by the insight of Black psycholgists, one can begin to understand how vitally important the roles of individual and family therapists are in uncovering and interpreting the content of African Americans' inner experience. The point needs to be made that in the absence of collective psychological approaches to the African American psychological dilemma, we can at least understand the nature and gravity of the situation through the presenting problems of individuals and families—multiplied many times. Clearly, racial oppression and discrimination result in feelings of rage, depression, self-alienation, low self-esteem, shame, desperation, hopelessness, and victimization. These are deeply felt psychical experiences for many African Americans.

---

[64] Ibid., 108–20.

CHAPTER 5

Black Psychology and African American Literature

Black writers seem always involved in moral and/or physical struggle, the result of which is expected to be some kind of larger freedom. Perhaps this is because our literary tradition is based on the slave narratives, where escape for the body and freedom of the soul went together, or perhaps this is because black people have never felt themselves guilty of global, cosmic sins.

Alice Walker

In the course of the discussions in the previous chapter around the development of theory and practice in the field of Black psychology, various aspects of the historical psychological experience of African Americans have been named and acknowledged. Yet, in terms of internal experience, simply to name and/or define a feeling serves only to interpret the experience in a generic sense. For example, to say that African Americans have had and are known to experience feelings of *rage* as a result of racial oppression serves only to provide a label to a kind of feeling. It does not serve to describe the feeling that leans more toward an interpretation of the experience that is contextual. Therefore, consistent with the assertion that the best form of knowledge for theory building is the experience of the context, the intent of this section is to give some description of the psychical experience of African Americans and the accompanying behavior that is incidental to the experience of slavery and racial oppression built into the current structures of American society. Basically, the description of the experience *as felt* internally is relative to the nature of the external experience and its impact on internal awarenesses. This kind of description is not readily available in the literature of Black psychology. Not only does the field need more literature along the lines that Jones and Boyd-Franklin have directed their work, but there is a void when it comes to sufficient descriptions of the African American existential dilemma in psychological terms.

In the absence of psychological literature that adequately describes the African American psychical experience in terms of the effects of the trauma of racial oppression on the development of the personality, other literary materials in the African American tradition may serve to provide descriptions.[1] For the purposes of this book, selected works of African American authors Toni Morrison and James Baldwin are quite appropriate for a brief introduction into the African American literary tradition as a resource for interpreting the psychological experience of African Americans. Both authors write about historical America from the African American perspective, and both are celebrated for their ability as fictional novelists to be able to put themselves into their writings and intuit what the real, lived experience must have been. It is conceivable that the success of Baldwin and Morrison, in part, has to do with the fact that they themselves are indigenous to the African American context, or in other words, products of the African American experience. This gives them a unique kind of awareness enabling them to write with clarity and believability, which those outside the context do not have the benefit of.[2]

---

[1] bell hooks, *Yearning: Race, Gender, and Cultural Politics* (Boston: South End Press, 1990), 225–30.

[2] James Baldwin and Toni Morrison have both received numerous awards, including Pulitzer awards. Toni Morrison is also a recipient of the Nobel prize.

Toni Morrison

Toni Morrison's ability to create fiction that is true to historical facts and to express it in such a way that it can be *felt* by the reader makes her work an excellent resource for the purposes of this book. According to author and literary critic bell hooks, Morrison's writing "evokes the passion of trauma during slavery as it carries over into black life when that institution is long gone."[3] Morrison's work gives insight into the psychological experience of Blacks during and after slavery. In particular, Morrison's book *Beloved* is an excellent fictional novel that, in psychological terms, leads to an understanding of how slavery traumatized the African psyche and shaped the African American personality thereafter.[4]

Briefly, Morrison's story revolves around multigenerational female characters, primarily, who contend with motherhood and trying to keep some semblance of family life, while confronted with the vicious system of slavocracy designed to destroy family and kinship ties. The title, *Beloved*, is also the name of an infant female child killed by her runaway slave mother, Sethe. Sethe had actually intended to kill all of her four children rather than see them enslaved for the rest of their lives. But Beloved is the only child that was actually killed before Sethe was apprehended. The story tells of the chain of events in Beloved's family leading up to her infanticide and its aftermath. Told in the first person of each character, the women—Sethe (Beloved's mother), Baby Suggs (Beloved's grandmother), and Denver (Beloved's sister)—are the primary characters. These women lament the anguish of their lives as the ghost of Beloved laments the anguish of her premature death. The Black men of the extended family from "Sweet Home" plantation, with the exception of Paul D. (Sethe's new lover, who passes through these women's lives again), are absent from the scene. In Paul D.'s words, they are all victimized one by one, including himself:

---

[3] hooks, 226.

[4] Although *Beloved* is fictional, its inspiration comes from a true story of a slave mother who killed her child. See Toni Morrison, *Beloved* (New York: Alfred A. Knopf, 1993).

One crazy, one sold, one missing, one burnt and me lick-
ing iron with my hands crossed behind me.[5]

However, in the case of Halle and Sethe's two sons, Howard
and Buglar, their reason for running away when they were old
enough to make it on their own was because of their ghost sister
Beloved's haunting presence in their house. Skillfully,
Morrison's way of telling the story allows the reader to see into
the mind of a woman who could do such a horrible act. The
reader is able to understand that prior to that eventful moment,
when Sethe slashed her daughter's throat, she had already endured more than she could take. She had been sexually assaulted
in the sixth month of her pregnancy, having her milk sucked
from her breasts while a note-taking school teacher and his students discussed her animal and human characteristics; she had
been badly beaten later the same day (leaving marks that re-
sembled a tree in her back) because she had released her children to go with a woman who would take them to freedom
while Sethe went back to look for their missing father; she had
never found her husband; alone, she had run for her own freedom; she had given birth to another child en route—while ex-
tremely sick, isolated, hungry, and without food. Yet she finally
made it to her mother-in-law's house and was reunited with
her children in freedom. Then, after a mere twenty-eight days
of freedom, Sethe recognized those whom she knew had come
to return her and her children to slavery coming into her mother-
in-law's yard. She was determined they would not go. Her mind
was made up.

Flashing ahead eighteen years after the horrible event,
Morrison describes the look of Sethe's eyes through the character of her soon-to-be-lover, Paul D:

Even in that tiny shack, leaning so close to the fire you
could smell the heat in her dress, her eyes did not pick
up a flicker of light. They were like two wells into which
he had trouble gazing…they needed to be covered, lid-
ded, marked with some sign to warn folks of what that
emptiness held.[6]

---

[5] Ibid., 72.
[6] Ibid., 9.

These are the eyes of a young girl whose mother was pointed out to her from among a line of women in a field. And between that vision and the vision of her own daughter, mutilated and dying by her own hand, Sethe's eyes had seen too much pain and sadness. At this point, Paul D. sees that emptiness is a dominant feeling in Sethe. Speaking to her Beloved, at her graveside, Sethe laments the moment that the emptiness arrived on top of pain and sadness:

> When I put that headstone up I wanted to lay there with you, put your head on my shoulder and keep you warm, and I would have if Buglar and Howard and Denver didn't need me because *my mind was homeless* then.[7]

Thus, at the start of each day, Sethe began the "day's serious work of *beating back the past*"[8] because "every mention of her past life hurt. Everything in it was painful or lost. She and Baby Suggs had agreed without saying so that it was *unspeakable*."[9]

A range of feelings and emotions are illuminated by Morrison through the character of Sethe's mother-in-law, Baby Suggs. Baby Suggs—the once strong matriarch of the family and self-made preacher and pastoral caregiver of unchurched slaves—dies outraged by all the unspeakable pain and sadness that she and her family had to endure as a result of slavery and all that it entailed. Regardless of the fact that her son Halle was able to buy her freedom in the later years of her life— "when it didn't mean a thing"—regret dominates her thoughts.[10] Not knowing at the time what had happened to prevent her last son, Halle, from arriving safely with Sethe and their children, Baby Suggs laments all the losses of her life: the losses of her other seven children, whom she believed dead, and the giving of herself until she had no self. "Sadness was at her center, the desolated center where the self that was no self made its home."[11] And years later, lamenting everything that has happened in her life including the dreadful sight of her daughter-in-law killing her own infant child (Baby Suggs' son Halle's child—Baby

---

[7]Ibid., 204
[8]Ibid., 73.
[9]Ibid., 58.
[10]Ibid., 23.
[11]Ibid., 140.

Suggs' own grandchild) as well as the torment by this child's ghost since, Baby Suggs remarks that "her past had been like her present—intolerable."[12] Finally, shortly before her death, Baby Suggs announces the essence of her rage:

> Those white things have taken all I had or dreamed…and broke my heart strings too. There is no bad luck in the world but whitefolks.[13]

Morrison's character Denver illustrates what it is to live in loneliness and constant fear. Denver is not only afraid that her mother's rage will return to harm again, but she becomes fearful of venturing outside the yard and as a result lives alone with her mother, yet in a world where she is isolated unto herself. Denver's inner feelings are illumined as Morrison describes her place of safe space—"a tree room" in the forest:

> First a playroom (where the silence was softer), then a refuge (from her brothers' fright), soon the place became the point. In that bower, closed off from hurt of the hurt world, Denver's imagination produced it's own hunger and it's own food, which she badly needed because loneliness wore her out. *Wore her out.*[14]

Last but not least, Morrison's character Beloved, the ghost of the murdered baby girl, elucidates a trauma of slavery not easily grasped—the senseless loss of life and that life's yearning for itself. This young lost soul is so full of outrage by the loss of her life that it "wept, sighed, trembled, and fell into fits."[15] An interesting slant in Morrison's story line is that Beloved's desire for life and sense of injustice is so strong that she manages somehow (perhaps with the unspoken desires of her mother and sister) to take on flesh and reenter the world to pick up her life with her mother and sister.

In terms of the psychical experience of African Americans, Morrison's words in *Beloved* have literally drawn pictures of

---

[12] Ibid., 4.
[13] Ibid., 89.
[14] Ibid., 28–29.
[15] Ibid., 29.

inner trauma that many slaves may have experienced. According to Morrison, the effects of slavocracy's trauma are extreme "sadness," described as a "desolate center" of a person; "rage" so strong it is unrelenting even in the face of death, or likened to a ghost's ability to return in flesh from the world beyond; "hurt" so deep that it is "unspeakable," causing one to completely remove oneself—to become empty inside so as not to feel anything; daily "denial" to prevent the past from being acknowledged in the present, and so on. Although Morrison's descriptions have to do with the consciousness of slaves (who were often good at employing defense mechanisms to protect their psyches), there is also a looming concern in the background for the negative psychical consequences in the collective unconsciousness of the genetic descendants of slaves (African Americans).

Another novel written by Morrison (actually her first novel), *The Bluest Eye*, demonstrates Morrison's ability to describe psychological content of African Americans in more contemporary times. In terms of Black psychology it imparts wisdom about internalized oppression and its effect on the African American psyche.[16]

Briefly, *The Bluest Eye* is a story that revolves around the tragic life of a young Black girl named Pecola Breedlove during the forties in Ohio. On top of all Pecola's unfortunate family dynamics, which have left her feeling very insecure and unloved, her sense of self-esteem is all but nonexistent in view of her earliest indoctrinations in grammar school. In school, Pecola encounters the White supremacy worldview that dominates society. This worldview has its way of devaluing everything about her blackness. Pecola has no way of knowing that society's rejection of her, even reinforced in the Black community, is a result of racism. Her response, however, is to begin to think that, if her appearance were more acceptable in society's view, her life would be happier. As a result, Pecola becomes obsessed with changing her appearance so that she looks like the "Jane" she had read about in her first grade primer. Jane and her brother,

---

[16] Toni Morrison, *The Bluest Eye* (New York: Holt, Rinehart, and Winston, 1970; reprint, New York: Plume, 1994).

Dick, the primer reads, had a perfect house and a perfect, happy family life:

> Here is the house. It is green and white. It has a red door. It is very pretty. Here is the family. Mother, Father, Dick, and Jane live in the green-and-white-house. They are very happy. See Jane. She has a red dress. She wants to play. Who will play with Jane? See the cat. It goes meow-meow. Come and play. Come and play with Jane. The kitten will not play. See Mother. Mother is very nice. Mother, will you play with Jane? Mother laughs. Laugh, Mother, laugh. See Father. He is big and strong. Father, will you play with Jane? Father is smiling. Smile, Father, smile. See the dog. Bowwow goes the dog. Do you want to play with Jane? See the dog run. Run, dog, run. Look, look. Here comes a friend. The friend will play with Jane. They will play a good game. Play, Jane, play.[17]

Of course, the primer's pictures illustrate the words, but also the unspoken words. Jane is pictured in her red dress, but clearly Jane is also pictured as a little White girl, who has blonde hair and blue eyes. Hence, Pecola unwittingly deludes herself into thinking that if she cannot change her skin color, at least she can change the color of her eyes; if only her eyes were blue—the bluest of blue—her life would be perfect too.

Morrison keeps Pecola's obsession and growing delusion in front of the reader. The words of the primer introduce the reader to the mindset formed early in Pecola's life. Yet Morrison prepares the reader for what is to come by writing these words in three stages. First, the words of the primer are arranged in sentences that are clearly punctuated. Then, there is no punctuation between the words. Finally, there is no distinction between the words at all as they all run together. Morrison also uses segmented sentences from the primer, without punctuation or spaces between them, as chapter headers, constantly alerting the reader to Pecola's blurred state of mind.

---

[17] Ibid., 4.

Sadly, there is nothing in Pecola's immediate world to challenge the worldview of dominant culture. In fact, the worldview of the dominant white culture has permeated the culture of the ghetto in which she and her family live, affecting the mindset and behavior of her parents as well as the sentiments of their neighbors.

> No one could have convinced them that they were not relentlessly unlucky and aggressively ugly. Except for the father, Cholly, whose ugliness (the result of despair, dissipation, and violence directed toward petty things and weak people) was behavior, the rest of the family—...Mrs. Breedlove, Sammy Breedlove, and Pecola Breed—wore their ugliness, put it on, so to speak, although it did not belong to them. The eyes, the small eyes set closely together under narrow foreheads. The low, irregular hairlines, which seemed even more irregular in contrast to the straight, heavy eyebrows which nearly met. Keen but crooked noses, with insolent nostrils. They had high cheek bones, and their ears turned forward. Shapely lips which called attention not to themselves but to the rest of the face. You looked at them and wondered why they were so ugly; you looked very closely and could not find the source. Then you realized that it came from conviction, their conviction. It was as though some mysterious all-knowing master had given each one a cloak of ugliness to wear, and they had each accepted it without question. The master had said, "You are ugly people." They looked about and saw nothing to contradict the statement; saw, in fact, support for it leaning at them from every billboard, every movie, every glance.[18]

Notably, although Pecola is Morrison's central character, she is characterized as passive in most situations. Cleverly, this is Morrison's way of demonstrating that it would be quite natural to assume that Pecola's kind of self-loathing makes her feel

---

[18] Ibid., 38–39.

that no one really cares what she thinks or feels. Whenever Pecola is asked her opinion or what she would like to do, her usual answer is, "I don't care." Hence, most of the story is told retrospectively, from the perspective of one of Pecola's former foster-sisters, Claudia MacTeer. Pecola's role is mainly to obsess about her ugliness and acquiring those blue eyes that will make everyone love her.

> Long hours she sat looking in the mirror, trying to discover the secret of the ugliness, the ugliness that made her ignored or despised at school, by teachers, and classmates alike...Each night, without fail, she prayed for blue eyes.[19]

In the meantime, as society's cruelty continues, Pecola takes her comfort in gazing at drinking cups with Shirley Temple's face smiling back at her with blue eyes, and candy wrappers with blued-eyed Mary Jane's face on them. The more extreme the external circumstances are that are forced upon her (such as the incestuous rape by her father, which resulted in a still-born child and the harsh gossip that followed), the more delusional Pecola becomes in defense of looks of revulsion (even from people who looked like her) toward the blackness of her skin. By the story's end, Pecola has lost all her sense of reality as she wanders looking through garbage in the streets.

The story about Pecola's self-loathing and obsession with dominant White society's image of beauty is a description of one of the most detrimental and oppressive psychological disorders experienced by far too many African Americans— internalized racism. The story has an extreme outcome. A person's whole life is lost. Yet the reality is that Black children in this country begin with this kind of orientation in their developmental years—an orientation that tells them that they are inferior, they are ugly, they are unwanted, and so on. Sadly, the orientation is reinforced throughout our lives in subtle ways, perpetrated mainly through the media (television, magazines, billboards, movies, etc.) and even through other Black people

---

[19] Ibid., 45–46.

in our families and communities who have in turn succumbed to external oppression and internalized it.

James Baldwin

James Baldwin's work is an excellent resource from which to glean psychological interpretation of the Black experience in America. His writing style is conversational, written in the voice of the first person, whether he is writing autobiographical material or nonfiction. In his fictional mode, like Morrison, Baldwin's characters are very true-to-life. I have selected Baldwin's work to illustrate that interpretations of the psychological experience of Black people in this country can also be gleaned from nonfictional literature in the Black tradition. Baldwin's last book, *The Price of the Ticket*, published shortly before his death, is a compilation of Baldwin's autobiographical works—be they essays or books in their entirety. It is approximately seven hundred pages of prose about his life observations. Basically, *The Price of the Ticket* is a historical documentary that details Baldwin's personal history amid his accounts of, and responses to, America's history in the making.[20] To say that Baldwin had the ability to describe the inner essence of Black people's experience in America is an understatement. In this regard, Baldwin's way with words, like Morrison's, was an extraordinary talent. Regarding his own life, Baldwin was willing to express some of his deepest thoughts, feelings, and emotions as well as expose telling intimacies. It appears that he was able to see into the thoughts and innermost feelings of others through the lens of himself, especially the perspective of Black men. For this reason, I have selected two quotes to interpret the experience of Black men (including his own) from three different generations. The first autobiographical excerpt is taken from Baldwin's *The Fire Next Time*, and the other from *No Name in the Street*:

> I certainly could not discover any principled reason
> for not becoming a criminal, and it is not my poor,
> God-fearing parents who are to be indicted for the lack

---

[20] James Baldwin, *The Price of the Ticket: Collected Nonfiction 1948–1985* (New York: St. Martin's/Marek, 1985).

but society. I was icily determined—more determined, really, than I knew then—never to make my peace with the ghetto but to die and go to Hell before I would let any white man spit on me, before I would accept my "place" in this republic. I did not intend to allow the white people of this country to tell me who I was, and limit me in that way, and polish me off that way. And yet, of course, at the same time, I *was* being spat on and defined and described and limited, and could have been polished off with no effort what ever. Every Negro boy—in my situation during those years, at least—who reaches this point realizes, at once profoundly, because he wants to live, that he stands in great peril and must find, with speed, a "thing," a gimmick, to lift him out, to start him on his way. *And it does not matter what the gimmick is.*[21]

It was an old black man in Atlanta who looked into my eyes and directed me into my first segregated bus. I have spent a long time thinking about that man. I never saw him again. I cannot describe the look which passed between us, as I asked him for directions, but it made me think, at once, of Shakespeare's "the oldest have borne most." It made me think of the blues: *Now, when a woman gets the blues, Lord, she hangs her head and cries. But when a man gets the blues, Lord, he grabs a train and rides.* It was borne in on me, suddenly, just why these men had so often been grabbing freight trains as the evening sun went down. And it was, perhaps, because I was getting on a segregated bus, and wondering how Negroes had borne this and other indignities for so long, that this man so struck me. He seemed to know what I was feeling. His eyes seemed to say that what I was feeling he had been feeling, at much higher pressure, all his life.[22]

---

[21] Ibid., 341.
[22] Ibid., 189–90.

There are volumes in these two excerpts in the same way that it has been said that "A picture is worth a thousand words." There is so much going on between Baldwin's lines as the reader imagines the scene and the characters described in words. The context of the first scene is inner-city life in the crime-filled streets of New York. Baldwin considers the very real dilemma facing growing Black boys as they come to realize the barriers and limitations placed on their existence by a racist society that will only tolerate them to a certain extent. Baldwin indicates through his own experience that there is a precise instance when it becomes clear to the average Black male youth that the evils of this society would just as soon "polish them off" (exterminate them) given the first opportunity that they put themselves in a compromising position. To be involved in criminal activity is to compromise one's self, but all too often, according to Baldwin, crime is the only "gimmick" that a young Black boy can identify to have some semblance of independence. Other avenues are blocked to them. Baldwin relates the "inner terror" that is felt in an instance and acknowledged daily as growing Black boys and men grapple with their desire to live and the reality that they are an endangered species.

The context of the scene of the second excerpt is the segregated South. Traveling from the North to the South, Baldwin as an adult has his first encounter with segregation in his travels. This brief encounter with this elder Black brother (not a biological brother but "a kindred" because he is a Black man in America too) forces Baldwin to consider all that these older Black eyes have seen in the days and nights of his Southern life. "How many times has the southern day come up to find...a black man, sexless, hanging from a tree!"[23] Baldwin acknowledges that between Black men there is a knowing that is shared without words of what it means to be a Black man in this country. Yet, for all the outrage that Baldwin feels, he must also acknowledge that this elder's outrage must far outreach his own. There is no way to compare the injustices that they have experienced in their different lifestyles (separated by years of experience and geographic locations). But there is still the rage. Baldwin

---

[23] Ibid., 189.

understands that Black women and men have always done what they had to do to survive, that our elders have endured more than some of us can imagine, but at extreme psychological expense. Baldwin knows that for many Black men, leaving their families was not the easy way out. It was just as hard to leave as to stay. This old brother had stayed. Baldwin has suggested that the "blues" are not always sung; sometimes they can been seen in the eyes of our Black elders.

Conclusion

African American literature provides insight into the psychological experience of African Americans. Authors such as Toni Morrison, James Baldwin, and Alice Walker (whose work was highlighted in chapters 1 and 3) have devoted their skill and writing talent to telling the African American story in ways yet to be recognized. These selections illuminate the African American experience so that it can be felt. Most importantly, these kinds of sources are reliable secondary resources that communicate effectively the inner experience of African Americans. In retrospect, the above sources confirm the nature and origin of the psychological oppression of African Americans and describe the nature of the conscious and unconscious inner response. Therefore, these sources also confirm that there is a crisis in Black Americans that is also psychological in its manifestation.

CHAPTER 6

A New Paradigm for
Pastoral Theology

*Whether we begin with paradigms created by mentors of
European and European American ancestry or with theoretical constructs emerging from the oral traditions in the
African Diaspora or with a dialectical, syncretistic inter-
play between the two, we must answer the inescapable
questions of appropriation and reciprocity.*

Katie Geneva Cannon

The African American cultural context requires that we address the critical survival and liberation needs of African Americans. This chapter will draw upon the sources in preceding chapters to discern implications for the construction of African
American pastoral theology. Theoretical implications begin with
the significance of linking sources that are indigenous to the
African American context and are vital for the construction of
pastoral theological method. Second, as a result of this inquiry,
this chapter will expand the discussion begun in chapter 1 concerning the components of a new paradigm for the field of pastoral theology in general and the African American context in
particular.

Cognate Resources Indigenous to the Cultural Context

As mentioned earlier, the significance of relying on sources that are indigenous to the African American context is that they are apt to interpret the African American cultural experience more accurately than the traditional sources of dominant American culture. It is significant that prior to this study a careful correlation of Black theology and Black psychology had never been conducted using existing pastoral theological method. Although the African American sources in pastoral theology to date are admirable attempts to bring the African American context into the pastoral theological dialogue, they have been limited in their ability to address the serious life-threatening communal concerns of African Americans because of their dependency on traditional sources of White dominant culture and approaches to pastoral theological method. It is impossible to conceptualize a framework for African American pastoral theology primarily from White sources. Inasmuch as cognate sources of traditional Western theology and psychology are deficient for the African American context by themselves, it is, indeed, time that the field of pastoral theology and care examine cognate sources that are indigenous to the African American context for their contribution to a conceptual understanding of Black experience in America.

Thus, for the purposes of this book, the cognate sources used to interpret the African American cultural experience have been selected from the literature of African American theology (Black liberation theology and womanist theology), Black psychology, and supplemental sources in the African American literary tradition. Attention has also been given to the implications of a methodological approach of these sources for the construction of a paradigm for African American pastoral theology.

Black Theology and African American Pastoral Theology

Black theology is essential to the enterprise of African American pastoral theology in the same respect that Hiltner asserted that pastoral theology is "an operation-focused branch of theology which begins with theological questions and concludes with theological answers."[1] In particular, the logic-centered (as Hiltner referred to systematic theologies) theologies of Black liberation theology and womanist theology raise the essential questions that speak to the communal needs of African Americans from the perspectives of Black men and women.

Therefore, unlike Hiltner's understanding, in which pastoral theology is *not* a link between operation-centered theology and logic-centered theology,[2] this book asserts that pastoral theology in the African American context should serve as a link to African American theology. That is, pastoral theology in the African American context should provide the link to the logic-centered theologies of Black liberation theology and womanist theology because of their conceptual understandings of African American experience.

It is quite significant that the earliest conceptions for the systematic constructions of Black liberation theology and womanist theology were outgrowths of the Black freedom struggle; both are grounded in the religious tradition of the Black church. Clearly, once African American experience became the focus of theological reflection, a creative outflow resulted that is responsive to the existential reality of African Americans.

In light of the realities of Black existence in a White racist system, Black liberation theology's intent is to empower Black people. The God language of Black liberation theology encourages Black people to image God as Black like them; that is empowering. It is also liberating because it frees us from the oppressive image of the White God of Western Christianity who sanctioned slavery, and whose response to slaves, in essence, was "The best way to be a good Christian is to be a good slave." The Black God of Black liberation theology's message to the oppressive circumstances of Black life in America today is "God is a God of the oppressed." Therefore, just as God was present with those oppressed in biblical times, God is also present in the Black struggle for freedom. Womanist theology is a

---

[1] Seward Hiltner, *Preface to Pastoral Theology: The Ministry and Theory of Shepherding* (Nashville: Abingdon Press, 1958), 24.
[2] Hiltner, 23.

counter-balance to Black liberation theology. For all practical purposes, the womanist tradition in theology seeks to restore wholeness and healing for the entire African American community—inside and outside the church. The womanist tradition reflection seeks to eradicate paternalism, racism, sexism, classism, or any kind of oppression in theological reflection. Thus, its point of departure is the experience of Black women. Therein lies the key to a communal approach that is holistic. Faith articulated in the womanist tradition speaks in terms of God as identified with the "least," as a divine cosuffer, and "God is able."

As the field of pastoral theology seeks to develop guidelines and strategies for pastoral caregiving in the African American context, it needs to reflect upon the same kinds of questions posed by African American theology. That is, in the practical sense, what does it means to be identified with the oppressed, to suffer with the "least"? What is meant by "God is able" in praxis?

Finally, the theological categories of *survival* and *liberation* call for a serious approach to the issues facing African Americans and, therefore, imply a moral ethic. Thus, the question of moral content of pastoral care for African Americans needs also to be considered at length. My intention here is to acknowledge the relevance of the question concerning the moral content of pastoral care in the construction of African American pastoral theology for future study. The need for moral ethics is implied in African American theology. Some argue that systematic Black theology is a branch of ethics. For the African American context, I have come to the conclusion that it is not a question of whether theology is a branch of theology or a branch of ethics. It is not an either/or question in the African American context. In terms of pastoral theology, the care needs of African Americans require that theological reflection on human dynamics and reflection on the moral questions must work together.[3]

---

[3] Religious ethicists whose works are excellent sources for further study on the issues of survival and liberation and ethics in the African American context are Katie G. Cannon, Theodore Walker, Jr., and Peter J. Paris, to name a few. See Katie G. Cannon, *Black Womanist Ethics* (Atlanta: Scholars Press, 1988); Theodore Walker, Jr., *Empower The People: Social Ethics for the African American Church* (Maryknoll, N.Y.: Orbis Books, 1991); Peter J. Paris, *The Spirituality of African Peoples: The Search for a Common Moral Discourse* (Minneapolis: Fortress Press, 1995).

Black Psychology and African American Pastoral Theology

As the field of Black psychology continues to develop, there are two primary implications for the enterprise of constructing African American pastoral theology. First is its phemonenological approach as it searches for understanding of the conscious development and self-awareness of African Americans. Second is the connection that Black psychology makes between African philosophy and the psychological well-being of African Americans. An intentionality on the part of many Black psychologists to recover a collective self-awareness of the *African self* is essential to the psychological healing and well-being of African Americans. In this respect, Black psychology's approach is also holistic. It seeks to reclaim and restore the African self to the American self of Blacks. Thus, it aims toward healing the dichotomy—the felt "two-ness"—that W. E. B. Du Bois spoke of and that many African Americans have been unable to reconcile.

As the field of pastoral theology seeks to construct African American pastoral theology, it needs to understand the psychological implications of being African and American. Therefore, it is my contention that African American pastoral theology should provide a link to Black psychology as a part of its method. Implicit throughout the psychological discussions in chapter 4 is the understanding that the clinical methods of Black psychology need to find ways to equip and empower African Americans psychologically to resist and cope with the influence of American society's negative aspects (past and present). African American pastoral care needs to do likewise.

Integral to the search for solutions to the psychological dilemma of African Americans—the search for survival and liberation—is an integrative approach that incorporates multisystems and embraces the benefits of the recovery of African beliefs and value systems. However, most challenging for the field of Black psychology, and, ultimately, the construction of African American pastoral theology, is the need to identify a method that is communal in approach. Certainly a family systems approach is a step in the right direction. The first order of a communal approach is to acknowledge the critical and urgent need in Black America. The second order then is to address a means to coordinate systems to work together for the collective good of African Americans.

Of the sources discussed in chapter 4, those pertaining to African-centered thought and Black psychology give important information that serves to interpret the experience of slavery and how the retention of African philosophy helped to sustain African Americans psychologically and spiritually throughout slavery and still today. The discussion on personality development and Black psychology addresses the negative psychological effects of traditional Western psychology in the experience of African Americans and speaks to the need to identify theories of positive determination for African American psychological functioning. The discussion on clinical intervention and Black psychology provides helpful insight into the contemporary psychological experience of African Americans and sets forth helpful guidelines for intervention with Black families that are quite useful to the field of pastoral theology. Notably, Black psychological theories for clinical practice in the African American context are beginning to incorporate and make use of African philosophy in their strategies for intervention with Black families. Finally, other literary materials from the African American literary tradition have served to fill a void in the literature of Black psychology as they illuminate the psychical experience of African Americans, past and present.

In terms of the African American psychological experience, all of the literature attests to the negative effects of slavery and racial oppression in this country and the communal need to find methods to address the issues. Clearly these are valuable secondary resources for constructing an African American pastoral theology. Also, all of the literature attests to the healing, sustaining, guiding, nurturing, empowering, and liberating benefit of recovering African cultural heritage and values to the enterprise of Black psychology and, ultimately, African American pastoral theology.

Linking Black Theology and Black Psychology

Integrating Black theology[4] and Black psychology is essential to the construction of African American pastoral theology. Making links between Black theology and Black psychology is somewhat different from Hiltner's approach. Hiltner's purpose for correlating the perspectives of existential theology and traditional depth psychology was to make comparisons and to use the perspectives as correctives of each other.[5] However, for the purposes of African American pastoral theological method that is holistic—and that provides for the goals of survival and liberation—the approach must be more than dialogical. It is essential that Black theology and Black psychology be integrated in the formation of conceptual theories for African American pastoral theology. Their integration helps us to understand the African American context because they speak to the social and psychological realities of Black experience through the perspectives of their disciplines.

Generally speaking, as it stands in the African American context, Black liberation theology serves to ground Black psychology, while womanist theology serves to ground both Black liberation theology and Black psychology. Specifically, the conceptual origins of Black liberation theology and Black psychology are quite compatible because their earliest conceptions focused primarily on survival and liberation from *racial* oppression. Womanist theology, on the other hand, conceptualizes the multidimensional need for liberation from

---

[4] For the sake of this discussion, I am referring to both Black liberation theology and womanist theology whenever I use the term *Black theology*. In the same way that I have interchanged the terms *Blacks, African Americans, Africans in America*, etc., the term *Black theology* can be interchangeable with *African American theology*. The intent is to convey that I am referring to theology that is indigenous to the African American context. It also should be noted that, while I am advocating that Black liberation theology and womanist theology are essential to the enterprise of African American pastoral theology that is sensitive to the survival and liberation needs of African Americans, that does not exclude other kinds of systematic approaches to Black theology—particularly approaches that incorporate African philosophy.

[5] Don S. Browning, "The Influence of Psychology on Theology," in *The New Shape of Pastoral Theology*, ed. William B. Oglesby, Jr. (Nashville: Abingdon Press, 1969), 132.

oppression found in Black women's experience (racism, sexism, classism, etc.) as well as survival and wholeness of life issues for the entire African American community. Although Black psychology has yet to advance developmentally to meet the kind of sophistication of systematic Black theology,[6] its attention to African philosophy and heritage brings preslavery considerations into the survival and liberation of African Americans.

Hence, pastoral theology in the African American context that is holistic and communal in approach requires that natural connections between Black theology and Black psychology be made and held firmly in pastoral theological reflection. The next section will discuss the implications of integrating Black theology and Black psychology for the survival and liberation of African Americans in terms of (1) the content of the communal experience of African Americans, (2) the recovery and retention of African heritage, (3) pastoral ministry, and (4) the aspects of ministry.

The Communal Experience of African Americans

The act of linking theology and psychology that is indigenous to the African American context accounts for both the existential and phenomenological kinds of questions that need to be addressed in order to deal with the survival and liberation issues of African Americans. Specifically, the inquiry of Black liberation theology and womanist theology into African American experience raises the existential dilemma of cultural oppression for theological reflection: What is God's message for the human conditions of Black men and women in the struggle for survival and liberation? The inquiry of Black psychology into the experience of African Americans seeks to understand the psychological experience of Black Americans: What accounts psychologically for the capacity of African Americans to survive and become liberated? In terms of survival, it is (1) the ability of African Americans to resist systematic

---

[6] Notably, the womanist school of thought needs to be strengthened in Black psychology so that the intent to address all of Black women's experience, along with racism, is incorporated into the construction of a method for the structuring of positive psychological functioning for African Americans.

oppression and genocide and (2) self-recovery from the psychological abuse of all kinds of oppression. Nihilism and genocidal poverty in Black America are the two greatest threats to the survival of African Americans as a people. In chapter 2, despair and hopelessness in the Black community was described as a nihilistic threat to Black survival resulting from generations of sustained racial oppression. (Clearly, this country has failed to live up to the full promises of democracy and does not promise to change much in the future.) The ecomonic oppression of African Americans seemingly contributes to a more gradual form of genocide that has taken place since slavery's end. Thus, African American pastoral theology and care must provide hope in view of the existential dilemmas of African Americans, both psychologically and materially.

The integration of Black theology and Black psychology provides hope for both dilemmas. Despairing African Americans can find hope and sustain themselves spiritually in the belief that the God of Black liberation theology is identified with our struggle to be free from our oppressions. When there seems to be no hope for an immediate way out of circumstances, there is hope in knowing that the God of womanist theology is identified with even the very "least" in the struggle and "is able to make a way out of no way." Black psychology, in the truest sense of the meaning, is engaged in the Black struggle for survival as it identifies the strategies of our African ancestors to sustain us even in the face of nihilism.

In terms of liberation as (1) total freedom from all kinds of oppression and (2) the ability to self-determine, the oppressive structures of American society must be addressed by African American pastoral theology. Together, Black theology and Black psychology point to an African American pastoral theology that must be prophetic in praxis. Clearly Black liberation theology and womanist theology are political theologies with the intent to empower African Americans in the face of their oppression. The intent to empower Black people collectively is accomplished by posing existential questions that are communal in nature and by liberating African Americans from theological methods and interpretations that have served to reinforce our oppression.

Black psychology, in turn, addresses liberation as it searches for a method that will enable African Americans to free themselves from the negative effects of psychological oppression in American society. Thus, African American pastoral theological reflection entails reflecting on the survivalist and liberative aspects of Black theology and Black psychology.

Recovery and Retention of African Heritage

The sources examined in chapters 3, 4, and 5 reflect a general consensus among Black theologians, Black psychologists, and authors of the Black literary tradition that the horrific experience of slavery has left an indelible imprint on the collective psyche of Black Americans. The psychological sources give evidence to a general opinion among many Black psychologists that slavery was the genesis of the negative psychological functioning in African Americans (carried over the generations). There is also a general belief that the oppressive racial climate that still exists in this country contributes to the negative psychological functioning evident in the behavior of many African Americans today. At the same time, there is also a growing awareness in the field of Black psychology that (1) many elements of African philosophy have been retained in African American culture, and (2) the retention of African philosophy in the psychology of African Americans has been integral to our positive psychological functioning. Another growing awareness is that the retention of African philosophy has reinforced our ability to resist the negative psychological effects of our oppression. Black psychologist Kobi Kambon expresses this awareness in the following passage:

> [It] should not be surprising to us that the basic emphases on the intricate relationships between kinship and community, social affiliation, shared participation and communal experience, religious symbolism and spiritual association are fundamental in the lifestyle of people of African descent throughout the world. Whether African people are observed in Africa, North and South America, or elsewhere, these ontological features are

viable and true to their African source. Thus, our music, our song, our vibrant and deeply-felt emotionality, our religious fervor, and our fundamental moral temperament all attest to the fact that there is such a phenomenon as the African personality defining the African psychical reality in North America and throughout the African diaspora.[7]

Thus, the significance of recovering and retaining African philosophy and heritage for the survival and liberation of African Americans is central to pastoral theological reflection.

Notably, as we consider the integration of theology and psychology that is indigenous to the African American context for the purpose of constructing African American pastoral theology, it becomes clear that linking theology and psychology is consistent with an African worldview that sees religion and philosophy as the same phenomenon. That is, the African worldview acknowledges a natural connection between theology and psychology inasmuch as the integration of Black theology and Black psychology allows for the unification of Black religious tradition that is incorporated in Black liberation theology and womanist theology, and the African philosophy that is incorporated in Black psychology. This is particularly significant if we are to seriously consider what benefit recovering and retaining African cultural heritage offers for the survival and liberation needs of African Americans. Hence, making the links between Black theology and Black psychology is a very practical consideration, conceptually.

Pastoral Ministry

The integration of theology and psychology that is indigenous to the African American context implies that the pastoral ministry in the African American context requires a communal approach. Clearly, to address the critical care needs of African Americans facing survival and liberation issues, the face of

---

[7] Kobi Kazembe Kalongi Kambon, *The African Personality in America: An African-Centered Framework* (Tallahassee, Fla.: NUBIAN Nation Publications, 1992), 15.

ministry in the African American context must change. Instead of one male face (who may be seminary trained) filling the pulpits of churches around the country, the wholistic[8] approach of womanist theology calls for many faces, male and female, fulfilling many roles of ministry in many places (churches, clinics, the community, etc.) throughout the country.

Together Black theology and Black psychology reveal that the experience of the African American context calls for staffs of ministers in every church who are preachers, teachers, and pastoral psychotherapists, too, if African Americans are to survive and become free of their oppressions, both spiritually and psychologically. In terms of the existential concerns that are material and encompass the *survival of all the people* as well as liberation from oppression, congregations must become part of larger ecumenical systems and networks that advocate for issues that are socioeconomic and political in nature.

A wholistic communal approach for the survival and liberation of African Americans also embraces the African concept of "spiritual oneness." Therefore, it does not discriminate against those who are unchurched or those who belong to other religious faiths (such as Islam, Judaism, Buddhism, etc.). This means that the mission field begins right outside the church door and concerns itself with the survival and liberation of all African Americans, regardless of their specific religious affiliations. Pastors in the African American context need to identify and facilitate the pastoral gifts of lay members in their congregations and coordinate those gifts with networks and systems beyond the church.

Finally, critical care of African Americans, especially poor Black women and their children, also requires that pastoral caregivers be advocates for survival and liberation. That is, in addition to Hiltner's "solicitous concern," the approach to ministry needs to include an *attitude of advocacy* for "the least of these" who are struggling with survival and liberation issues.

---

[8]I intentionally use the term "wholistic" rather than "holistic" to denote womanist meaning as distinguished by Jacquelyn Grant to acknowledge a tradition that declares that God is at work in the experience of Black women.

Aspects of Pastoral Ministry

Womanist theology acknowledges that poor single Black women and their families are the "least of the least" because they are the "poorest of the poor" and the most "oppressed of the oppressed" in view of the racism, sexism, and classism that usually accompanies any other kind of oppression that may exist in American society. The "least" are those who continually stare nihilism and genocidal poverty in the face and require urgent, attentive, critical care for survival and liberation. Thus, the aspects of pastoral caregiving must expand beyond Hiltner's "healing, sustaining, and guiding." As we have seen through the integration of Black theology and Black psychology, the intent of care must be also be *nurturing, empowering,* and *liberating* if African Americans, collectively, are to survive the harshness of their external realities and the duress of their psychological realities as well.

Nurturing, in view of the struggle for survival and liberation, entails constant pastoral caregiving for indefinite periods of time that enables one to gain enough strength to raise one's self up amidst the struggle. *Empowering* entails putting people in touch with their own power so that they are enabled to claim their rights, resist oppression, and take control of their own lives. *Liberating* ministry entails action, including political activism, that works toward the elimination of oppression.

Additionally, in light of the potential of African cultural heritage for healing, sustaining, guiding, nurturing, empowering, and liberating African Americans spiritually and psychologically, it is also incumbent upon pastoral theology to reflect upon *reconciling* ministry in a new light.[9] In this respect, reconciling in the African American context is an act of reclaiming, restoring, and retaining African philosophy and culture in ministry to African Americans. Reconciling in this respect is also an act of reconciling African Americans to African Americans. That is, reconciling middle-class African Americans to under-class

---

[9] Until such time as there is a genuine interest in the larger American society for reconciliation of the alienation between Whites and Blacks resulting from the societal wrongs done to African Americans as a whole, survival and liberation requires that African Americans concentrate on reconciliations that bring healing and wholeness within the African American community.

African Americans,[10] and reconciling that eliminates fratricide among African Americans, which has reached epidemic proportions. This is a vital element in the survival and liberation of African Americans.

In conclusion, pastoral theology in the African American context provides theological theory that has resulted from theological reflection on the experience of African Americans. This study has integrated theology and psychology that is indigenous to the African American context for the purpose of interpreting the Black experience in America. The perspective of poor Black women determines that *survival and liberation* require pastoral caregiving in the African American context, which includes functions that are also *nurturing, empowering, liberating,* and *reconciling.*

These aspects will be discussed in detail in chapter 7. The next section of this chapter discusses the implications of the paradigm shift that is tailored to the communal needs of African Americans, yet is viable for other cultural contexts as well.

A New Paradigm

The new paradigm presented here is not exclusive to the African American context and is valid for a communal approach to any cultural context. Basically this paradigm is a revision in pastoral theological approach to allow for cultural particularities and to accommodate a communal approach.

Pastoral theology is "a subsystem within theology in general, and practical theology in particular."[11] To underscore the importance of cultural contextuality, we might define pastoral theology as theological reflection on the experience of the cultural context that is relevant for strategic pastoral caregiving in the context of ministry. Therefore, the task of pastoral theology—regardless of cultural context—is to develop theory and practice for culturally sensitive strategic pastoral caregiving. As

---

[10] I give credit to Dr. Homer Ashby, Jr., of McCormick Theological Seminary in Chicago for introducing the need for reconciliation between the middle- and lower-class Blacks as a concept of Black pastoral theology during a workshop presentation at a Society of Pastoral Theology convention.

[11] Larry Kent Graham, *Care of Persons, Care of Worlds: A Psychosystems Approach to Pastoral Care and Counseling* (Nashville: Abingdon Press, 1992), 23.

stated in chapter 1, an approach that accommodates this definition of pastoral theology requires (1) that the point of departure for theological reflection be the experience of those who inhabit the cultural context, (2) that the pastoral caregiver's experience be regarded as secondary to the experience of the cultural context, (3) the discernment of an *umbrella perspective* that combines the cultural perspective and the pastoral perspective for the practice of ministry, and (4) revisions in our understanding of the crucial aspects of ministry. The following sections discuss the implications of these four components of the paradigm shift.

The Experience of the Cultural Context

The field of pastoral theology must become aware that knowledge is relative to cultural awarenesses. It is also essential that comprehensive contextuality take precedence over the more narrow shepherding approach in order that the most accurate account of the historical, social, cultural experience of those inhabiting the context of ministry is presented for theological reflection. Experience of the context as the point of departure for theological reflection for the African American context is an existential/phenomenological approach adapted specifically to the contextual needs of African Americans. It acknowledges that the people indigenous to the context are the subjects of their own stories rather than the objects of projections and/or perspectives formed by other worldviews. In terms of the African American experience, assumptions that presume to know social location by appearances distort the African American reality. The greatest mistake is to assume that the African American experience is monolithic in any respect. It is, however, true that a common experience of all African Americans, regardless of social location, is the experience of racial oppression in one form or another. After all, the basis of our oppression in this country was racial in the first place, and that remains true in contemporary times. There are a multitude of stories of lived experience in the African American context depending on socioeconomic factors and the level of acculturation or assimilation of dominant European American ideology. Whether dealing with individuals, families, or communities, an awareness of the historical background, social location, and personal experience of culture is essential in providing guidelines for wholistic care. For any context, it is necessary to get in touch with the reality of the cultural experience if the pastoral approach is to prove effective for that culture's pastoral care needs. Therefore, it is best to get firsthand knowledge of the experience as interpreted by those who actually live in the context. Usually, for purposes of formal research, ethnographic or qualitative studies are employed to access the reality of a culture's experience. However, neither approach would be easily managed in an effort to study a community that spans the nation's continent.

This contextualized historical approach employs secondary resources to access and manage information about the African American context. African American history, sociological data on African Americans, Black theology, Black psychology, and African American literary materials are the secondary sources used to interpret African American experience. However, a historical approach in any context could make use of sources that are indigenous to the cultural context (including ethnographic and qualitative studies as well as sociological, theological, psychological, and other data) in addition to historical data. It is also instructive to note that theology is central to pastoral theological method and that psychology offers a great deal of insight into the experience of the context. Other secondary sources will serve to correlate and augment these primary sources. The intent is to get as true a picture of the cultural experience as possible. Most significant is that sources that are indigenous to the cultural context are most sensitive to the cultural particularities.[12]

The Experience of the Pastoral Caregivers

To consider reflection on the pastoral caregiver's experience as a second step in pastoral theological method does not negate

---

[12] Christie Neuger took this approach to build a pastoral theology that is sensitive to women. See Christie Cozad Neuger, "Feminist Pastoral Theology and Pastoral Counseling: A Work in Progress," *The Journal of Pastoral Theology*, vol. 2, Summer, 1992.

the importance of the pastoral caregiver's perspective. On the contrary, it strengthens the validity of the pastoral caregiver's perspective. Pastoral care persons who take time to inform themselves and to reflect on the particularities of the cultural experience of the context in which their ministry is situated will be better prepared to form a perspective that is accurately representative of the needs of the constituents in the ministry context.

The shift in the paradigm from the pastoral caregiver's experience as the point of departure to the experience of the cultural context lessens the potential of imposing the pastoral caregiver's perspective. In the African American context, pastoral caregivers have often imposed their own values and assumptions on African American experience rather than trying to understand the subjective experience or honoring the significance of values and issues specific to the African American worldview.

In general, new and different contexts should be viewed by the dominant culture as learning situations rather than approached as situations in which the pastoral caregiver imposes his or her own perspective. Therefore, pastoral caregivers who are not indigenous to the cultural context of their ministry should involve themselves in additional self-study or training situations that are instructive of the cultural context.[13] Without this kind of preparation, the pastoral perspective provides little usefulness, because in most instances it will not reflect the realities of the ministry situation. In this respect, a perspective without accurate supporting information amounts to nothing more than a biased or unfounded opinion.

I will use myself as an example. I write as an African American woman, pastoral theologian, and pastoral psychotherapist whose clinical practice focuses on the African American context. I work primarily with African American women and their

---

[13] This creates a need with which those in the field must come to terms. In general, doctoral programs need to come to terms with issues of postmodernism, as do training centers or internships that are intended to prepare those entering the field of pastoral counseling. In the meantime, pastoral theologians and other pastoral caregivers need to be intentional about acquiring knowledge that equips them with the tools necessary to approach contexts different from their own.

families who are economically oppressed. This provides me with a personal awareness that makes me more knowledgeable about the experience of the African American context than many of my colleagues in the field of pastoral theology and care. At the same time, however, this formal inquiry into African American experience through historical and sociological data, Black theology, Black psychology, and other sources indigenous to the context has increased my own awareness of the oppressive nature of African American experience. Therefore, I am quite confident when I assert that understanding the perspective of poor Black women is a means toward understanding the nature of the crisis in Black America, and that a womanist approach points toward strategic pastoral caregiving that is wholistic.

Another important implication of this shift in point of departure from the experience of the pastoral caregiver to the experience of the cultural context is a recognition that there is no guarantee that those doing the theological reflection have come to terms with their own issues and biases prior to forming their perspectives. For example, the paternalism inherent in traditional pastoral theology has overprized the role of the pastor's perspective and is therefore limited in its ability to understand the African American context. This brings me back to a question that I asked at the beginning of the study: Whose pastoral theology is it? Inasmuch as traditional pastoral theology represents the dominant cultural perspective, the appropriate answer to the question is that pastoral theology belongs to the culture that generates it. This will undoubtedly be the case, if the perspective of the cultural context takes precedence over the perspective of the pastoral caregiver. For example, the primary focus of traditional pastoral theology has been limited to theological reflection on the pastor's perspective of problems such as "illness, death, sexuality, family, and personhood" in the ministry situation.[14] Yet the critical issues of African Americans, collectively, poses a problem of far more serious proportions for theological reflection. Therefore, the concepts of *survival*

---

[14] J. R. Burck and R. J. Hunter, "Pastoral Theology, Protestant," in *Dictionary of Pastoral Care and Counseling,* ed. Rodney J. Hunter (Nashville: Abingdon Press, 1990), 867.

and *liberation* are introduced as viable constructs for pastoral theological reflection in the communal context of Black America.

Discerning an Umbrella Perspective

The concept of an *umbrella perspective* came out of the search for a communal approach to the African American problem. Yet it has utility for pastoral theological method in any cultural context, especially when the approach is communal. Discerning an umbrella perspective—a perspective that combines the worldview of the cultural experience with a pastoral care perspective—serves to provide an umbrella over the acts of ministry and points to appropriate strategies for pastoral caregiving. In other words, the umbrella perspective acknowledges the cultural problem that pastoral caregiving needs to address.

For example, in terms of the African American context, I have asserted that the most appropriate umbrella perspective at this time is the worldview of poor Black women, because it encompasses the multidimensional oppression of African Americans as a whole. Hence, if pastoral care is to adequately address the urgency of the situation facing poor Black women, it must develop strategic pastoral caregiving for African Americans that is wholistic. Therefore, in the African American context, every act of ministry should identify with and respond to the critical cultural problem of African Americans—survival and liberation.

Revising the Aspects of Ministry

The fourth component of the new paradigm is that it is provisional. It allows for updates in the functions of the ministry in light of the pastoral care needs of the context of ministry at the time. A paradigm that begins with theological reflection on the experience of the cultural context is likely to expand or revise traditional pastoral theological method. Depending on the umbrella perspective that represents the experience of the cultural context and the pastoral caregiver's perspective, the strategies for the content of ministry are likely to be different from healing, sustaining, and guiding in some way. It may only be that new aspects are added to the functions of ministry. For example, an umbrella perspective for the African American context of poor Black women calls for ministry that is also nurturing, empowering, liberating, and often reconciling.

Conclusion

For the African American context, the resulting shift in paradigm, along with the integration of Black theology and Black psychology as a means of interpreting the African American experience, comprises a method that corrects and expands upon the traditional paradigm of pastoral theology.

In general terms that are corrective in nature, this shift in paradigm accommodates the need for a communal approach, cultural sensitivity, and the elimination of the paternalism and individualism that are inherent in the traditional paradigm. In terms of expansion, this paradigm shift builds on the significance of the human experience for pastoral theology, shifting its focus for theological reflection from the experience of the pastoral caregiver to the experience of the cultural context. It also expands Hiltner's interdisciplinary approach to include cognate sources that are indigenous to the African American context. Finally, this shift in paradigm has taken seriously Hiltner's charge that pastoral theology is a provisional and constructive enterprise. In light of the contemporary lives of African Americans, I have built upon provisions made for pastoral theology in a previous era. It appears that Hiltner's provisional concept has been lost or neglected, but the provisional nature of pastoral theology is the foundation of the tradition. Everything that I have asserted for the African American context at this time and the field in general is provisional or prefatory. Chapter 7 will present guidelines for strategic pastoral caregiving in the African American context.

CHAPTER 7

Pastoral Care for the African American Context

I tell you the truth, whatever you did not do for one of the least of these, you did not do for me.

Matthew 25:45 (NIV)

Strategic pastoral caregiving in the African American context must provide strategies that address the survival and liberation issues of African Americans. Therefore, it has already been established that the functions of ministry in the African American context need to be expanded beyond the traditional view of ministry as *healing*, *sustaining*, and *guiding* to include aspects that are *nurturing*, *empowering*, and *liberating*. The aspect of *reconciling* is also reconsidered as a strategic concept for the pastoral care of African Americans. The purpose of this chapter is to formulate guidelines for pastoral caregiving of African Americans.

In the Black religious tradition, I give honor to God for having made it this far in my own life, and to the ancestors and elders who have struggled over time to provide for the pastoral care needs of the African diaspora residing in America. It cannot be said that those who have preceded me have not given of themselves to find ways to nurture, empower, and liberate

129

African Americans to ensure the *survival of the people* and sweet *oneness* in freedom. In reality this book serves to affirm wisdom known for ages, which has gradually been forgotten for communal praxis.

As I begin to consider guidelines for the pastoral care of African Americans, I am aware that the desire to write a book like this is also in response to womanist urgings within me, endeavoring to be expressed to the field of pastoral theology and care and to the Black church. Notably, Black grandmothers and mothers have understood and strategized to provide communal care for the acute needs of African Americans struggling to survive and liberate themselves from oppression throughout the history of Black people in this country.[1] In this respect, I acknowledge that in writing this book, I have picked up the mantle of Black women who have struggled long before me with these same issues. In the final analysis, what results in suggested guidelines for pastoral care of African Americans— yet facing critical survival and liberation issues—comes unapologetically from a womanist perspective.

Other Exemplary Narratives of Black Women's Experience

At this point, it may be helpful to put two more faces of African American women in front of the statistics presented in chapter 2 to make the reality of the statistics come to life. The descriptions from their lives as African American women is presented to voice their critical care needs. Following the narratives are sections that discuss the implications of these narratives for the practice of pastoral care ministry to African Americans in general. The final section discusses strategies for pastoral caregiving from a Black church perspective.

A Wounded Healer...

Pauletta came into therapy seven years after her eldest son had been shot to death by a teenaged gang member simply because he was wearing the wrong colored hat (Pauletta's son,

---

[1] Katie G. Cannon, *Black Womanist Ethics* (Atlanta: Scholars Press, 1988), 66.

also a teenager, had not been a gang member). Her presenting problem was that she needed to process her grief in the context of her whole life. For the past seven years, instead of taking care of her own needs, Pauletta had been forced, more or less, into the role of bearing the grief and taking care of others who were too horrified to even talk about the reality of what had happened to her son. Thus, Pauletta was subjected to knowing looks and glances from others (very often church people) that acknowledged the horror that had entered her life the day her son was killed. These same people, however, resisted talking about the subject because they either didn't know how to talk about it, or they did not want to be reminded of it. Sometimes, when Pauletta introduced the subject of her son's untimely death, there were also looks suggesting, "Here we go again. We've heard the story before. Can't you move on?" As a result, Pauletta's primary role was often to reassure everyone that she was strong enough to handle it.

When Pauletta initiated therapy, she was also feeling a lot of guilt because she felt that her younger son had to grow up in the shadow of his older brother's murder. She also had fear about what the future held for him and for her. The younger son was then preparing to join the military, and Pauletta needed to be able to release him to his own life and put her own life in perspective.

The first step (and only step as it turned out) in our sessions together toward processing the event, seven years previous, was purging all the grief that preceded her son's murder as well as that which followed. In addition to living through every Black mother's worst nightmare, the murder of a child, Pauletta held a lot of grief around many of the dynamics of her own personal life in general. Life as a Black female had by no means been easy for Pauletta, in her roles as a school-aged child, a single parent, an entrepreneur, and so on. After the news of her son's murder left the limelight, she had not experienced much support from anywhere. Pauletta admitted that she had probably had and recovered from several nervous breakdowns in solitude.

The purging went on session after session, but it was what she needed. That was not what was needed to solve her problems, but there was an enormous amount of grieving that Pauletta had to come to terms with before she could move on with her life. Much of it has had to do with living the socioeconomic realities described in chapter 1 as a single Black mother. Currently, Pauletta is doing fairly well; she is involved in work that she enjoys as a community activist.

One Who Has Defied All Odds...

Into her early forties, Doris wonders how long she will hold up physically. As it is, her health is so poor that she is physically unemployable for most jobs that her level of education and training will allow her to work. Most of her life, Doris has been abused in one way or another. The initial abuse was unintentional on her mother's part. Because Doris' mother was away so much working several jobs, she was a strict disciplinarian whose philosophy was "I would rather beat my own kids to make them act right, than for them to get beat out in the street by White police." During the times that Doris was left with her older siblings, the brutality of their beatings was sometimes much worse than her mother's.

Although Doris is able to understand her mother's intentions and forgive her, she also recognizes that it was the physical and emotional abuse in her own household and her awareness that she, as a Black female, was not valued in society that resulted in her self-abuse through alcohol and drugs. Drug and alcohol abuse began early in Doris' life and continued until recently.

Doris also feels that she has endured extreme psychological abuse by the social agencies that she has had to contend with because she and her two children receive public assistance. She has a daughter and a son who are both hard of hearing. After Doris had brought her children through the difficult years before anyone knew how badly impaired the hearing of both of her children was, social workers seemed ever present, monitoring her every move, while threatening to take her children away at their slightest whim. It is interesting that representatives of these social agencies had to rely on Doris in order to communicate with her children, but they were concerned about her ability to care for them. She was humiliated and disempowered in front of her children.

For several very intense years, Doris and her children lived with the constant fear that they could be separated from each other. Then social workers were forced to acknowledge that Doris was a capable and loving mother and that they had no legal recourse. Doris still lives with the fear that the "System" (as she refers to the network of the social agencies) will find ways to intrude upon their lives again, at any point in the future, as long as they receive public assistance.

Doris was referred to me by an African American woman who had facilitated court-ordered therapy group of which Doris was a member. It was this therapist's opinion that Doris benefitted from her membership in the group (Doris agreed), but she felt that Doris also had some other issues for therapy once the group terminated. Doris had grown attached to this African American counselor and trusted her, but she was resistant to her suggestions for further counseling, especially if the counselor was White. There was also the problem of money. If this African American woman had not been resourceful, creative, and persistent, it is likely that Doris would not have been in therapy beyond that point. The therapist was able to identify some funds to get Doris started in counseling with me.

When the money ran out, we continued. The issues were too serious to drop. I was aware of Doris' deep-seated fears and concerns about the future, and I had witnessed some of her trauma during our visits that were in her home. In reality, Doris spent most of her time at home child-rearing, in the silence of two deaf children, trying to negotiate the "System" and struggling with poor health, while people (even church people) and family distanced themselves from her and her children. I could see that Doris, despite all that she had been through, was still trying to overcome the odds without any real support. Doris was virtually alone.

Discussion

There are some striking commonalities among the narratives of these three African American women (including Lemonine, whose story was shared in chapter 1). First, the lack of an economic base that erodes the quality of life on so many levels affects them all.[2] There was undue stress connected to the fear that life might get worse than it already was in all three stories. The mental duress connected with economic oppression was quite draining for all three women. The toll that this stress has had on the physical health of Lemonine and Doris was quite evident. Lemonine reached physical exhaustion trying to make ends meet, and ultimately she died of a malignant brain tumor. I do not profess to be a medical doctor, but a direct connection between stress and cancer is widely accepted. Despite the fact that Doris' poor health may be, in part, a result of the alcohol and drug abuse or the physical abuse that she suffered as a child, her most prevalent health concern is her chronic asthma, which also is generally connected with emotional distress. In any case, Doris' health problems are indirectly connected to the lack of an economic base beginning as far back as Doris' mother's need to work several jobs.

Second, the kind of desperation and hopelessness that resulted from sustained situations of extreme duress is evident in each story. Having known Lemonine in the context of therapy, I am convinced that after years of quiet despairing, in the end she gave up hope that things would ever really change. She finally became silent on the subject of hope, for she had none. Pauletta's son's senseless death is indicative of the magnitude of hopelessness in the larger Black community that has resulted as the many forms of racial oppression over time have taken their toll on one's ability to hope for brighter days ahead. One

---

[2] I am concentrating on the experience of African American women who are at or below the poverty level because economic oppression is a critical factor in the needs of African Americans to survive and be liberated. However, for those who would like to know about stories of middle-class African American women's experience, I recommend an excellent resource work on the subject by Kesho Yvonne Scott. Scott shares the narrative of five middle-class African American women (including herself) and their perspectives as they reflect on their survival strategies for life in American society. See Kesho Yvonne Scott, *The Habit of Surviving* (New York: Ballantine Books, 1991).

manifestation of the nihilism in the Black community is fratricide—young Black boys killing each other because life as it is
experienced has no meaning or value to them. Therefore, it is
nothing to take another life, especially if the other person represents the self that is hated because of internalized racism. Thus,
the destructive cycle continues, affecting innocent people who
have no basis for understanding why. I am thankful that, at the
present, Pauletta is still hopeful and seems to be finding ways
to cope, but it is not easy to do. Doris struggles to have hope,
even though she can see little hope in the realities around her.

These stories reveal that these women are alone in the face
of their troubles much of the time, while others look to them for
nurture and support. The care that they sought through pastoral counseling was intended to fill the void in their lives created by the absence of a support network. Where was/is God
in all that they go through on a daily basis? They were reaching
out for God's care, desiring to realize its evidence in their lives.
Therefore, pastoral theology and care in the African American
context must be representative of the voices of poor Black
women declaring that God is at work in their experience, too.

Guidelines for Pastoral Care in the African American Context

The goal of African American pastoral care is to adequately
address the critical care needs of African Americans, from the
perspective of poor African American women, to ensure the survival and liberation of African Americans as a whole. In other
words, pastoral care for African Americans requires caregiving
that addresses the crisis that we face in terms of survival as a
people and liberation from all kinds of oppression.

At the onset of this book's inquiry, one of the many questions that occurred to me was, Whose problem is it that the situation of African Americans is so critical? I could not resolve in
my own mind that the magnitude of the crisis in Black America
appeared virtually overlooked by the field of pastoral theology
and care until recently—until African American religious scholars surfaced the concern. Therefore, this question needs to be
answered in the context of providing guidelines for pastoral
care of African Americans.

The gravity of these three African American women's experiences encompasses the experiences of other African American women like themselves, the majority of whom have not attained middle-class status economically, and the experiences of their family members—male, female, young, and old. In turn, these women's experiences also encompass the experiences of the Black community and touch the structures and systems of American society. Their experiences cannot be grasped as individual instances apart from the African American community and the larger contexts of American society.

Therefore, the pastoral care of African Americans is not just a situation that African American pastoral theologians and pastoral caregivers need to address. The existential problems confronting African Americans today are as much an American problem as the institution of slavery in this country was an American problem. Hence, the crisis in Black America presents a ministry situation that the field of pastoral theology and care needs to come to terms with, collectively. In other words, the communal pastoral care problem of African Americans is a communal concern for the field of pastoral theology and needs to be addressed by those in the field. I am not saying that it is the field's responsibility to single-handedly solve the problems that have been raised here. Instead, my contention is that it is incumbent on the integrity of the field, whose discipline is theological reflection for the purpose of guiding pastoral care, to acknowledge the crisis and take appropriate measures to address the issues as a discipline.

Answers to the other questions of When? and How? provide the content of guidelines for pastoral care in the African American context. These questions are answered from the perspective of poor Black women. As already mentioned, the perspective of poor Black women serves as an umbrella perspective that guides the pastoral care for the context of ministry in the Black community.

In general, guidelines for the pastoral care of African Americans from a womanist perspective call for the expansion in the character and content of the ministry described by Hiltner's shepherding perspective. In terms of the character of ministry, the womanist perspective offers two guidelines in addition to

Hiltner's call for an "attitude of tender and soliticious concern."[3] The first order of business for pastoral care of African Americans is that pastoral care must be willing to respond to the *urgency* of the needs in the African American context. In light of the narratives of these three Black women (that supports the sociological data presented in chapter 2), two of the most detrimental issues threatening the collective survival of African Americans and our ability to self-determine are *genocidal poverty* and *nihilism*. The immediate and long-term future of African Americans as a people hinges on an attention to the urgency of finding solutions that can help to change these situations. Time is very much of the essence in the answer to the question of When? There is no more time to waste by ignoring, denying, excusing, or just being overwhelmed by the problems of the African American context.

Second, the attitude of pastoral care should also be one of *advocacy* that is embodied in action. The attitude of the pastoral caregiver will have everything to do with how a relationship is entered into and developed in the process of caregiving in the African American community. Of utmost importance is genuine communication, on the part of those offering pastoral care, of empathy and concern that generates a clear intention of advocacy. In essence, the necessary message is that the caregiver identifies with the problems—that he or she mirrors God's identification with the "least"—and is committed to working through the problems. An attitude of advocacy will not only engender trust in relations within the African American community; it is the kind of support that is needed among African Americans who are trying to survive and self-determine. When we reflect on the narratives of Lemonine, Pauletta, and Doris, it is clear that they were in need of true advocates, not just persons who could give lip service to being advocates. They needed to connect with persons who believed in their struggles and struggled with them in a real way. There will be many occasions in the life of pastoral caregivers in the African American context when the role of advocacy is needed. The pastoral caregiver must follow through on the best of intentions in the larger context of society.

---

[3] Hiltner, *Preface to Pastoral Theology,* 16.

In terms of content of ministry, the womanist perspective calls for an expansion in the character and content of ministry described by Hiltner as "aspects of shepherding." As mentioned earlier, reflection on the exigencies of Black life in America should dictate the content of ministry. In light of the struggle for survival and liberation, aspects that are crucial to the function of ministry must go beyond Hiltner's healing, sustaining, and guiding. *Healing* will not come for African American poor people without liberation from oppressive systems that continue to keep the wounds of racism, sexism, and classism open. *Sustaining* is not enough in the face of critical issues that threaten the very *survival* of African Americans as a people. *Sustaining* should not be confused with *surviving.* Hiltner speaks of sustaining as "upholding," and "standing with"[4]—in other words, as *support.* Survival, in the communal sense for African Americans, entails much more than being sustained or supported through short-lived crises of individuals and families. African Americans need pastoral care to ensure their survival, not only of the day-to-day struggles of Black life in America, but also survival of the effects of more than four hundred years of oppression, dehumanization, and genocidal poverty.

Finally, *guiding* can only be helpful if the pastoral caregiver gives preference to the subjective implications of the cultural context of African Americans over his or her objective point of view. In other words, the pastoral caregiver must educate himself or herself fully about the cultural context before he or she can give any sort of guidance. Inasmuch as healing, sustaining, and guiding do not encompass the expressed need for nurture, empowerment, and liberation of African Americans or our need for reconciliation, these aspects must become integral to the acts of ministry in the African American context. In a formal sense the remainder of guidelines for pastoral care expand upon previous statements about nurture, empowerment, liberation, and reconcilitation from a womanist perspective.

Nurture. Pastoral care of African Americans should provide nurture. Although the word *care* is synonymous with the word

---

[4] Ibid., 69.

nurture, pastoral care as healing, sustaining, and guiding—altogether—has not managed to provide the distinctive kind of care that is also nourishing and restorative. The harsh conditions in Black America have been longstanding; some have been more harsh than others, and some are escalating in their intensity. For many African Americans there seems to be no end to the crises that tend to build on one another. This is coupled with the awareness that Black people, collectively, have already endured so much, for so long. To stay alive and to stay in the struggle, many African Americans need a constant source of care that restores and replenishes vitality for continued resistance of the external oppressive circumstances. Pastoral care that is nurturing must seek to understand what has already been endured in the lives of individuals and their families, and the collective struggles of African Americans. Thus, acts of ministry that are nurturing involve consistent care over long periods of time (sometimes a lifetime) in order to nourish and raise one up in the midst of a struggle for survival and liberation. Pastoral care must, then, find ways to hold and support those in its care throughout the tiring stages of crisis, until our struggle to move beyond the African American crisis is actually achieved.

Empowerment. Pastoral caregiving in the African American context should result in empowerment. To be *empowering* would be to find ways to give power to those disenfranchised, to enable persons to resist oppression on their own and to take authority over their own lives. People who are fully empowered do not have to struggle for power to survive or to self-determine their lives. People who are empowered are better able to resist oppression than those who are not; people who are empowered are able to help other people become empowered. To empower is to help people get in touch with the power that is theirs—to help them identify their power, claim their power, and/or to recover power that has been taken from them. Thus, pastoral care in the African American context needs to find ways to identify, coordinate, and facilitate power in the African American community.

Liberation. Survival and liberation of African Americans, as the ultimate goal of pastoral care, requires that pastoral caregiving be *liberating* in the political sense as well as the spiritual sense. Liberating acts of ministry would be those that work toward actually setting persons free from oppression. Without attention to the issue of liberation, there is no allowance for pastoral advocacy that helps to bring about the elimination of oppression.

Reconciliation. Finally, pastoral caregiving should be *reconciling*. I am of the opinion that the survival and liberation issues facing the vast majority of African Americans merit another look at the relevance of *reconciling* as an aspect of ministry in the African American context. The times are such that race relations between Blacks and Whites seem more strained than moving toward reconciliation. A case in point is the aftermath of O. J. Simpson's criminal and civil trials. Yet we have witnessed that President Clinton has made the first necessary step in reconciliation: an apology for the wrongs done to African Americans through slavery in this country. So, there is hope that one day reconciliation between African Americans and the greater American society may be possible. Yet, in all honesty, it would still appear to be a long way away. While I do affirm the validity of the arguments of Edward Wimberly and others regarding the relevance of reconciling for African Americans and greater American society at this point in time, I am of the opinion that in order to offset the nihilistic threat infringing upon Black life in America, African Americans need as a priority to reconcile ourselves with one another and with lost traditions and strategies for survival inherent in African culture.[5]

Specifically, it is vital to the survival and liberation of African Americans that we reconcile relations within the Black

---

[5] As well as to Cornel West, Vincent Harding, and Arthur Jones regarding the value of African heritage for the contemporary struggle of African Americans, I give credit to Homer Ashby, Jr. Ashby was quite instrumental in stimulating my thoughts in the direction of reconsidering reconciliation in a different light when he raised the question during a workshop presentation at the Society of Pastoral Theology in Chicago the summer of 1995. Basically, Ashby addressed the need to reconcile middle-class Blacks to under-class Blacks, the meaning of which I did not fully grasp at the time. Ashby also raised the importance of Afrocentric cultural knowledge for a Black pastoral theology. As I have considered the nihilistic threat to Black Americans, it has become increasingly clear that African Americans need to be reconciled to each other, and knowledge of our African heritage and culture needs to be restored to us.

community that, ultimately, reunite the upper and lower classes of African Americans with each other and reduce and / or eliminate fratricide among male youth in particular. African Americans also need to reconcile ourselves with the healing and sustaining wisdom of our African heritage. Further, pastoral caregiving that intentionally seeks on the behalf of dominant White culture to heal the alienation between Whites and Blacks is appropriate pastoral caregiving in the African American context.

In terms of concrete examples, these guidelines are intended to give guidance for communal approaches in pastoral care. Unfortunately, the kinds of examples that are needed are virtually nonexistent at this time and need to be developed. However, as an illustration of the kinds of networking that are necessary, I expand upon Doris' story. Again, the reader needs to read the narrative in light of the larger population of African Americans, because the numbers of men, women, and children who are confronted with these kinds of situations (and worse) throughout the African American community are of epidemic proportions.

My approach to pastoral care in Doris' situation is a clear example of how willingness and an intentionality of advocacy can result in pastoral caregiving that nurtures, empowers, and liberates at the same time. Reconciliation for Doris remains an objective because she has not been cared for in the community sense. One of the major concerns that I had for Doris was how debilitated and immobilized she became physically after her encounters with White persons representing the various institutions with which she had to contend. There were times when her relations with the school system created so much stress for her that she could not see past them. Whenever Doris shared with me how some of the teachers and administrators at her son's school treated her and her son with disrespect, she seemed to relive the negative feelings that resulted from the initial violations. Clearly, Doris' expectations were that these demeaning experiences would reoccur time and time again throughout her children's school years. As I listened to Doris, I could see the anguish that this caused her, but I also heard a dreaded resignation at the same time. Listening and hearing was not enough. It was clear that she needed someone to help her change this dynamic, if possible.

Therefore, I resolved that I would step into the role of an advocate. On several occasions, our sessions took on a different approach. In the place of one regularly scheduled session for counseling, I accompanied Doris to her son's school for a conference. Once we sat down with the principal and teacher, it was clear that just my presence with Doris changed the usual dynamics. Those who were used to talking to Doris (and perhaps others) in condescending and disrespectful ways found themselves trying to remember how to go about talking to another human being on equal terms. Doris felt supported enough in the new space that had been created to express her thoughts clearly and calmly. At the end of the conference, we all agreed that sometimes Doris' son was difficult, but that at other times, because he had been labeled as a "difficult child," misbehavior was automatically expected of him without giving him the benefit of the doubt. In essence, all I had done was to be present, announce who I was, and indicate that in the interests of Doris and her children I was concerned with her son's progress.

When I reflected on this event later, I was impressed with Doris' command of herself and the situation as she expressed herself at the school that day. I had not known what to expect, because whenever Doris had talked about these kinds of situations in our sessions, her voice had dropped to a whisper; that is how overcome she had been by the oppressive feelings of these exchanges.

This dynamic changed thereafter. Confident that she could count on my support, Doris approached me on another occasion to participate in a meeting between her and a social worker who had called to set up an appointment to offer her his services. Doris' concern was that, although it was supposed to be voluntary, she felt the intent was to intimidate her to agree to regular home visits again. Doris said she just needed some moral support. During a scheduled counseling session, I gave Doris moral support by sitting in the room and observing the conversation between her and the social worker. (However, consent forms for release of information had been signed in advance in the event that the worker wanted to ask me how things were going in counseling.) Again, Doris handled herself beautifully; she managed to stand up for herself and say, "Thanks, but no thanks."

Both of these instances of advocacy on my part served to give Doris the kind of support that had been missing most of her life—someone to advocate for her. Our relationship was strengthened as Doris experienced what it was like to have someone be willing to advocate for her as needed. Doris understood that I was an advocate for her. These acts of advocacy made Doris feel nurtured, enabled her to access her own power, and resulted in very liberating outcomes.

On a communal level, it is interesting that Doris often commented on how supported she felt in the counseling group with other women like herself. I tried to identify such a setting for her as we considered her options once we terminated, but to no avail. I wished many times that I had had the resourcefulness to create the kind of situation that Doris and so many Black women like her needed. Money was always the question.

On the larger scale, networks need to be put in place that interface with each other to accommodate Doris' needs and those of many others in the African American community who desperately need this kind of support. As it was, in Doris' situation, I became involved with the schools, social services, and the church. I even found myself counseling with Doris as I drove her to the Department of Motor Vehicles so that she could take her first driver's test ever. What does that look like on a larger scale? This is the kind of support that used to happen naturally in communities as people reached out to each other. It does not happen in many instances anymore, leaving people like Doris without the most basic kinds of support.

Therefore, the most concrete example of an approach to the pastoral needs in the African American context is that of a community that cares for all its members. In other words, a nationwide community of support networks needs to be created through which there is a concerted effort among churches, schools, social agencies, and other institutional resources to provide caregiving of African Americans that is *urgent*, *advocating*, *nurturing*, *empowering*, *liberating*, and *reconciling*. In reality, it is up to those of us in the field of pastoral theology and care—including the Black church as the primary system in the African American community—to strategize ways to bring the theory into practice. Literally, pastoral caregiving of African Americans takes on the role of advocacy for the complete survival and liberation of African Americans, *spiritually*, *psychologically*, and *physically*. The key word in the previous statement regarding a communal approach is the word *physically*. In light of African Americans' legacy of resiliency and resistance to oppression on the spiritual and psychological levels over time, the deciding factor for total survival and liberation of African Americans is in terms of *physical* survival and liberation.

Hence, to include the physical along with the spiritual and psychological well-being of African Americans implies politicization of the work of pastoral theology and care. This is essential if the critical issues of many Black Americans are to be solved. Those in the field of pastoral theology and care and those in the Black church must create a public will to address and eliminate systemic racial oppression. The next and final chapter discusses pastoral care strategies for the communal survival and liberation concerns in the African American context.

CHAPTER 8

Strategies for Pastoral Care in African American Communities

Black Theological social ethical reflection affirms that our churches, denominations, and various religious communities are uniquely qualified and morally obliged to offer diverse-unified-bread breaking-God-conscious leadership in social thought and action.

Theodore Walker, Jr.

The practice of ministry needs to be responsible and accountable to the theological theory. Unfortunately, in reality it appears that all too often, once the theoretical work is done and the time comes to put the theory into praxis, the old saying "Easier said than done" seems to rule. The result is praxis that usually falls short of intended goals. There is great danger of this happening in the African American context in view of the overwhelmingly complicated circumstances. However, the following strategies for pastoral caregiving for African Americans focus on a communal approach that has expediency in addressing the problems. They are directed at a communal approach for which we in the field of pastoral theology and care need to take some leadership. The leadership must be practiced in conjunction with the Black church and other societal systems in the interest of survival and liberation of African Americans.

An important first step in strategic pastoral caregiving for the African American context is an expedient acknowledgment by those in the field of pastoral theology and care of the severity and urgency of the crisis of many African Americans. In turn, those in the field need to commit themselves, as a community of pastoral theological reflection and pastoral caregivers, to interfacing with concerted societal efforts in responsible and accountable ways until survival and liberation of African Americans is no longer an issue.[1]

Second, as previously noted, this book was not intended to provide all the answers. Strategically, my hope is that this work will encourage those in the field to continue to make communal strides toward grappling with the complexities and the enormity of the pastoral care concerns of African Americans. Knowledge of the context as it is experienced and interpreted by sources indigenous to the context is a basic strategy of this model of pastoral theology.

As a third strategy, the field of pastoral theology and care needs to place priority on bringing the sensitive issues of racism and its pervasiveness out into the open. As a means of reconciliation, this would be much more than a dialogical exercise. Existing and newly created forums could be convened for the purpose of serious engagement with scholarship in the field and cognate fields that address race as an issue in caregiving professions and relations in this country. We must also encourage those willing to address racism as an issue in their scholarship and promote their work.[2] The intent is to raise the consciousness about the reality of racism and its oppressive effect on the quality of life for African Americans in

---

[1] Organizations such as the Society of Pastoral Theology, the American Association of Pastoral Counselors, and their respective journals can create the forums to raise the issues and concerns of the African American context to promote a public will for a collective response.

[2] For example, a colleague, Darryl Fairchild, is directing his doctoral work toward developing "psychological understanding of race and racial identity" from a White perspective that focuses on White racial identity formation. Also James Poling's work involving racial and gender oppression is a good example of how pastoral theological work has been directed toward race oppression. See James Newton Poling, *Deliver Us From Evil: Resisting Racial and Gender Oppression* (Minneapolis: Fortress Press, 1996).

contemporary times and to form networks that help to create a public will for racial justice and the eradication of racist systems and structures in society.[3]

Fourth, pastoral caregiving in general needs to take similar initiatives (like the initiative on race described above) for political strategies in spheres of influence to promote liberation from all kind of oppressions, such as sexism, classism, heterosexism, ageism, and so forth.

Fifth, recognizing that the Black church network is the largest and most influential system in the African American community, pastoral caregivers need to be intentional about interfacing with the efforts of the Black church network. The Black church is the arena through which most of the nurture, empowerment, liberation, and internal reconciliation of African Americans can result. The potential for pastoral caregiving is even greater with the concerted support of pastoral caregivers throughout American society. The intent is to identify resources and find ways to coordinate and distribute needed resources.

Notably, these strategies politicize the pastoral approach. In reality the situation is so critical in the African American context primarily because most of American society justifies looking the other way—including the White church, as well as disciplines of caregiving and religious studies. Further, nothing is going to change unless the public will is changed to bring about racial justice. In light of the crisis that festers in Black America, the question is, How long can a field whose discipline is pastoral theology and care avoid doing the right thing? Politics is a part of life in which we must engage; without political action there is no power to change anything. These strategies include the mobilization of political power into the praxis of pastoral caregiving. The following section discusses strategies for the Black church approach to pastoral care of African Americans. These strategies are more specific in nature.

---

[3] For recommended reading that frames the subject of racism and race relations primarily between Blacks and Whites, specifically for consciousness-raising, see Derrick Bell, *Faces at the Bottom of the Well* (New York: Basic Books, 1992); and Andrew Hacker, *Two Nations: Black and White, Separate, Hostile, Unequal* (New York: Ballantine Books, 1992).

The Black Church and Pastoral Care
of African Americans

Brother Pastor, Sister Pastor, it has been said that, in the Black religious tradition that came to this country with our African ancestors, the Black church has been the champion of the cause for survival and liberation of African Americans. Yet when I look upon the conditions under which the majority of African Americans live and die, I wonder where that church has gone? Why are there so many unchurched African Americans, and why are our youth taking their own lives,[4] when that is not the way it used to be when Black folk were in church? Could it be that we have somehow lost sight of the people for the church buildings we feel so compelled to build? Could it be that these structures, some so massive, are blocking our view of the mission field right outside the church doors? I gratefully acknowledge some remarkable Black church ministries around the country[5]; however, that does not negate clear evidence that the Black church is in crisis, as it fails to adequately address the collective survival and liberation issues of Black America. We need to ask and answer important questions. Then we must redress the problems of our community, because so many look to the Black church and still believe that it should be the champion of the cause for survival and liberation of African Americans.

The brief narratives of our sisters shared in previous chapters speak volumes to us in terms of the experience that we need to listen to, hear, and act upon immediately because they are us. No matter how large the Black middle class grows, none are free until all are free. A tremendously large underclass of African Americans live lives that resemble our sisters' or are much worse. As part of the solution, middle-class Blacks need to be intentional about turning around to bear with the "least

---

[4] The results of a study released by the Federal Centers for Disease Control and Prevention found that "the rate of suicide for black youth ages 15–19 had more than doubled, to 8.1 per 100,000 in 1995, from 3.6 per 100,000 in 1980. It found a similar pattern for ages 10–14…Suicide is now the third leading cause of death for Black 15- to 24-year-olds. "Suicide Rates Increase Among Black Teenagers," Denver Post, March, 20, 1998, 5A (Written by Pam Belluck of the *New York Times*).

[5] For examples, see Forrest E. Harris, Sr., and Donna E. Allen, eds., *A Call to Dialogue and Reflection On: What Does it Mean to be Black and Christian?* (Nashville: Kelly Miller Smith Institute, 1992), 18–22.

of these." The Black church, as the largest system in the Black community, can be instrumental in making that happen. We must also interface with others who are willing to join the Black struggle. The truth of the matter is that the Black church is still key to the Black struggle, but it has to acknowledge this collectively and redirect its praxis in the direction of the struggle.

Prior to implementing specific strategies for pastoral caregiving in the context of Black church ministry, we must do the work of getting the church house in order. Much of this kind of work serves to nurture, empower, and liberate Black people in and of itself. Three major concerns must be addressed in the process of putting our houses in order and reorientating toward a more productive course: (1) dealing with our sexism, (2) healing the schism between the Black church and Black religious scholarship, and (3) addressing the role of the pastor.

Sexism in the Black Church

The subject of sexism in the Black church is raised occasionally, but it is still as sensitive a subject as racism is in American society. It is easier said than done as Black male pastors give lip service to full equality of women but hold tightly to their role of authority in the tradition of the apostle Paul. Their congregations, including many women, hold to the same tradition. As a result, all too frequently, Black women pastors are still viewed as inferior to their male counterparts. Often women ministers are expected to minister for little or nothing, or there are significant disparities in the salaries of men and women. The men are usually paid more for the same position, sometimes even when the men have less preparation for ministry. Black women, in general, are more seen than heard as they continue to carry the church on their backs.

As I reflect on the narrative of Lemonine, I see a woman who felt rejected by the church. As she searched for a church home, Lemonine felt a lack of acceptance of the gifts she had to offer to the ministry of the churches where she visited. She felt that the essence of the message given to her was always the same: The male pastor would decide in good time when and where she could serve, after she had proven her commitment and loyalty to the pastor's leadership. It was clear to her that she was not welcome unless she learned how to play the pastor's game of church politics. Notably, while members of the church are becoming more aware that there is such a thing as Black theology, Black theology that is also womanist theology is almost unheard of by name, depending perhaps on the location in the country. Clearly, womanist theology expresses the need for the Black church to rid itself of sexism and oppression of any kind altogether.

> Such a theology will "allow" God through the Holy Spirit to work through persons without regard to race, sex, or class. This theology will exercise its prophetic function, and will "self test" in a church characterized by the sins of racism, sexism, and other forms of oppression.[6]

There are too many instances when Black churches cannot pass the "self test" in terms of the sin of sexism. How is it that sexism is still so prevalent, while we continue to preach that "God is not a respecter of persons"? The incongruence and the hypocrisy are glaring. We need to get our houses in order.

Schisms in the Black Church

The Black church as a whole needs to be unified. Various kinds of schisms in the Black church have occurred for one reason or another. It is possible that at the basis of some of the schisms are social class distinctions. That possibility could bring another kind of oppressive sin into view—classism—and that would be significant. Is this occurring when middle-class churches and lower-class ones cannot find ways to come together to minister to all of God's people?

Another major schism that I want to address in the collective Black church is the once very clear schism between the leadership (pastorate) of the Black church and Black religious scholars. In recent years there appears to have been some intentional reconciliation between the two factions. Many of the church leaders are seminary trained, and this has served to make

---

[6] Jacquelyn Grant, "Black Theology and Black Women," in *Black Theology: A Documentary History, Volume One, 1966–1979*, 2d and rev. ed., ed. James H. Cone and Gayraud S. Wilmore (Maryknoll, N.Y.: Orbis Books, 1993), 335.

way for the reconciliation. However, unless we are discussing large middle-class churches in the larger urban areas, it still appears that distinctions are made between "school theology" and "revelations from the Holy Spirit" in many of our churches. In the meantime, God's people are truly being destroyed for lack of knowledge. Too many are still captivated in their religious thinking by an image of a White God looking down on them. Too many even resist hearing the nurturing, empowering, and liberating messages of God expressed through Black liberation theology and womanist theology.

Clearly, the work of most Black religious scholars indicates that they have identified their gifts for ministry; most have focused their scholarship on the Black struggle for survival and liberation so that they could give back to the Black community. The Black church needs to receive these gifts as God's gifts to the collective benefit of the Black church. It makes no sense to allow this schism to remain. We must concentrate on finding ways to intervene in these circumstances to rectify this divide between church and scholarship. Our future as Black people depends on it. We need to get our houses in order.

The Role of the Pastor

In times past, perhaps we as a people could not have made it without the able leadership of pastors/shepherds willing to lead their folks through every toil and danger. There is much to be thankful for, but if you have been listening this far, please hear this too: Just as much as the shepherding perspective of traditional pastoral theology has lost its currency for the approaches to pastoral care in general, the autocratic pastor attempting to do the pastoring all by him or herself is an outdated role for the Black community. Plainly, people do not need to be led; they do not need to follow the shepherd around, because the shepherd cannot be there every time they have a need. The people need to be empowered to do for themselves, each other, and the pastor too. Black people struggling to survive need more nurture than one pastor can give. Black people need also to be freed from the bondage of this model of ministry. Who does it really serve effectively? If for no other reason than the fact that the needs are too great, the pastorate must view itself differently. The pastorate needs to be multistaffed. There needs to be a complementary mix of gifts among the senior pastor (facilitator/administrator) and associates that meets the ministry needs of the congregation and surrounding community.

Several years ago, I had the privilege of serving under a senior pastor who attempted to ensure that Jesus was truly at the head of the church. The philosophy of the ministry was this: If Jesus were truly the head of the church, the body could come together in working order. What a concept! Jesus at the head of the church! The scriptural basis was the fourth chapter of Ephesians[7]:

> It was he who gave some to be apostles, some to be prophets, some to be evangelists, and some to be pastors and teachers, to prepare God's people for works of service, so that the body of Christ may be built up until we all reach unity in the faith and in the knowledge of the Son of God and become mature, attaining to the whole measure of the fullness of Christ. (Eph. 4:11–13 [NIV])

Under the pastor's leadership, the congregation experimented with this concept until we found a viable approach. Initially the pastor (gifted as a pastor, preacher, teacher) facilitated a process through which church members were able to identify their personal gifts for the ministry. Eventually the lay leadership of the church was involved in the process of enabling others in the same manner. We called it "equipping the saints for ministry."

Ultimately, natural leaders for the various aspects of ministry were raised from the congregation. The process was prayer for guidance and nurture (preaching, teaching, counseling) until members felt empowered to acknowledge their gifts for ministry and respond to the call to serve in areas where they felt most

---

[7] On a personal note, I have long reflected on this epistle to the church at Ephesus, especially chapter 4, for its meanings for ministry. As an African American woman, it resonates deeply with me. Although some may think it humorous, it seriously occurred to me, long before I learned that biblical scholars had conceded that this epistle could have been written by someone other than Paul, that these were the words of a woman—perhaps someone who knew Paul's work, like Priscilla—because this is a womanist way of caring for the community.

gifted and akin. It was all voluntary as opposed to being coerced by the pastor to take on responsibilities because someone
had to do it whether they liked to or not. Positions on the church
council were filled in the same manner. As persons came for-
ward feeling called to serve in that capacity, they were elected
by support of the congregation. It was a beautiful situation in
which the outreach ministry to the community superseded beau-
tifying the facility or celebrating the pastor's anniversary in a
costly manner. This is not to say that those other concerns were
not addressed. There were plenty of gifts and lots of energy for
all kinds of ministry, but outreach was the priority. This church
grew from a small church to membership that multiplied in a
relatively short time span.[8] I mention this ministry because it
represents what one pastor was able to achieve with a congregation. This ministry represents empowerment of its members,
who, in turn, make it their primary priority to reach out and
provide care to the surrounding community. We need to get
our houses in order as this church did.

The Black church needs to come to terms with its crisis as a
church and reconsider its priorities. If the choice is to champion
the cause, the first priority is the survival and liberation of African Americans. Inasmuch as the Black church is the largest institution in the Black community, it is the focal point for the
direction and momentum that the struggle takes. Everyone will
be watching to see how the Black church responds, as we enter
the twenty-first century cognizant of the fact that many African
Americans live under conditions of genocidal poverty and have
lost hope for the future. My prayer is that the Black church will
get its houses in order and move ahead prophetically. The following sections provide strategies for nurture, empowerment,
liberation, and reconciliation in the practice of ministry through
preaching, pastoral counseling, Christian education, youth ministry, and community outreach.

Strategies for Pastoral Caregiving in the Black Church

The following strategies for pastoral caregiving in Black
church ministry are specific to the crisis in Black America. As I

---

[8] This was the ministry of Park Hill Christian Church (Disciples of Christ),
Denver, Colorado; pastor, Rev. Deborah Thompson.

have discussed, the role of the Black church is critical to the survival and liberation of African Americans. Again, urgency is paramount, and an attitude of advocacy is vital to strategic pastoral caregiving in the African American context. In the following discussion, I point to the potential in specific ministries of the Black church for survival and liberation strategies of pastoral caregiving. Therefore, the approach is not intended to be comprehensive. It is focused on the urgency and needs of the "least," although it is intended to benefit the whole Black community.[9]

Preaching

We have heard it said in the Black church that the preacher, in the preaching moment, must preach as if he or she is a dying man or woman, who is preaching to dying people. Sadly, this is a truth that we must contend with as we witness all the many and quick ways that death comes to the young as well as the old. Some do not want to hear that genocide is real in the Black community, but it is. Many Blacks are too weary to resist the oppressive forces that come against us anymore, and too many are despairing, without hope to carry on the struggle. Every action of the church needs to, as Theodore Walker, Jr., titled his book,[10] "empower the people." Thus, every message preached should send a message from God that "the hope is in the struggle." The struggle must continue because therein lies the hope that empowers.

The interpretations of Black theology are intended to lift Black people up, to provide empowerment, to nurture and provide food for the soul and energy for the daily struggles, to offer liberation from distorted religion and hope for the struggle ahead. We need to revisit the scriptures with a new eye for texts not often used that express the message that "the finger of God," as Allan Boesak titled his book,[11] is pointed at the oppression that we endure as Black people. We must reaffirm that God is present in the struggle with us and that we can receive God's

---

[9] For a comprehensive view of Black church ministry, see James H. Harris, *Pastoral Theology: A Black-Church Perspective* (Minneapolis: Fortress Press, 1991).

[10] See Theodore Walker, Jr., *Empower the People: Social Ethics for the African American Church* (Maryknoll, N.Y.: Orbis Books, 1991).

[11] Allan Boesak, *The Finger of God: Sermons on Faith and Responsibility* (Maryknoll, N.Y.: Orbis Books, 1982).

blessings if we are open to the truth of God's word, which will indeed set us free. We have grown accustomed to preaching and hearing God's word in an oppressive way, even when we have the best intentions.

Womanist theology has been with us all along. It has its eye on God's message to the "least of these," lifting up the women as well as the men, the poor as well as the middle class. Preaching that comes from "the heart of American Black culture," known as soul theology,[12] needs to take precedence in our preaching. Black preachers need to identify God's message to the people not only in the words of wisdom that have been handed down from our ancestors, but also in the wisdom of our own words. In this way, we can have a real conversation between God and ourselves through which Black people are nurtured, empowered, liberated, reconciled to God and each other, and offered hope for the struggle.

Pastoral Counseling

There appears to be some disdain in the Black church for counseling that is psychological in nature, mainly because of a lack of trust in Western psychology. There also appears to be a kind of possessiveness and reluctance on the part of many pastors to allow one's members to receive counseling (spiritual or otherwise) from anyone other than themselves. However, the truth of the matter is that every pastor who can preach does not come with the gift for pastoral care. Amazingly, very often it is the pastoral gift for ministry that has been overlooked in the ministry of the church, as we have focused on the pastor's ability to preach above all else.

Often, as Edward Wimberly points out, care and nurture in the African American church takes the form of story-telling and listening on the part of the pastor and members of the church. Usually the pastor initiates the context for ministry, yet it is the members who carry through in prayer groups and in other supportive contexts.[13] This is perhaps as close as we get to pastoral counseling in many churches.

---

[12] See Nicholas Cooper-Lewter and Henry H. Mitchell, *Soul Theology: The Heart of American Black Culture* (Nashville: Abingdon Press, 1991).

[13] See Edward P. Wimberly, *African American Pastoral Care* (Nashville: Abingdon Press, 1991).

What the Black church needs to recognize is that many of its people suffer tremendous psychological burdens. Although there are many possibilities as to why, there are two major reasons why the Black church needs to address the psychological aspects of persons along with the spiritual. First, psychological burdens may be caused by deep spiritual conflicts, often created by theology that is oppressive. Secondly, many suffer from psychological problems as a result of the physical and psychological oppression that we as a people have experienced for as long as we have been in this country. If African Americans are going to survive and be liberated, we must intentionally provide pastoral care that allows for counseling that addresses the psychological along with the spiritual.

This reality calls for pastoral care that includes counseling in the church for individuals, families, and groups on an ongoing basis. To accomplish this role, pastoral counselors need to be professionally trained pastoral counselors and psychotherapists. Formal preparation for counseling credentials is another kind of scholarship that provides gifts for ministry that must not be overlooked in the membership of the Black church.

Christine Wiley conducted a study on the impact of pastoral counseling in the Black church setting for her doctoral work.[14] Her model, which still functions, incorporates the gifts of professional counselors in the church into the church's ministry. Wiley's model is womanist in approach—intentional about addressing the multidimensional experience of Black women in order to encompass the needs of the whole church. The contribution of Wiley's study and model is that it demonstrates the benefit of approaching pastoral care through church-based counseling and affirms the need to bring the spiritual and psychological needs of Black people together in the church. This is consistent with our African heritage, which did not separate spirituality and psychology.

---

[14] Christine Y. Wiley, "The Impact of a Parish Based Pastoral Counseling Center on Counselors and Congregation: A Womanist Perspective" (D.Min. diss., Garrett-Evangelical Theological Seminary, 1994).

Christian Education

Christian education involves more than the study of scripture. Studying to show one's self "approved" also entails studying the circumstances around the scripture to put it into an appropriate context, past and present. For many African Americans, the question of identity in relation to the scriptures has been troubling, even oppressive. Therefore, it is especially important that Christian education and study of scripture entail knowing and understanding ourselves and our heritage in relation to scripture.

Christian education is the ideal situation in which to raise the consciousness of the Black church about the origins of its religious tradition, which are primarily African traditional, Jewish, Christian, and Islamic. This awareness is essential to the survival and liberation of African Americans because it restores vital knowledge that has been lost. Knowledge of scripture and our African heritage together brings a wholeness and healing, spiritually and psychologically, that African Americans have been in search of since we were taken from the motherland. In this respect, Christian education nurtures and reconciles as it empowers and liberates.

Youth Ministry

Our youth are our future. If we hope for real change in the future, the seeds need to be planted now. Therefore, the youth ministry of the Black church is vital to the survival and liberation of African Americans. As scripture says, our children need to be trained in the way that they should go. First, our youth need to be recovered from the streets and brought into the church or into settings where they can be exposed to the truth about God and the struggles that they face. It is going to take a lot of courage and determination, but we need to find a way to get to our children before they kill themselves or someone else. The killing has to stop!

In addition to the kind of instruction that is suggested for Christian education in general, we need to come up with curriculum for our youth that gives them the information that they will need to know in order to recognize oppression when it presents itself and to be able to resist and overcome. Based on the information that Black psychology is learning about the value of African philosophy and culture for positive psychological functioning, a strong suggestion is that the curriculum needs to be Afrocentric, providing for rites and rituals that are compatible with the various developmental stages. Then, in an urgent manner, the Black church needs a nationwide agenda for networking and implementation.

Community Outreach

The community is more than the church congregation. It is the whole Black community outside the church doors. It must include those who do not come to church, those who cannot come to church—"the least of these"—the sick, the old, the imprisoned, the poor, and so on. There are communities of people within the Black community who are immobile for the most part. The Black church needs to go to them. A primary example is the community of Black people (men and women) behind prison walls. Black people need to stop saying that there is a shortage of Black men (even if preceded by the adjective "viable"). There is not. Too many are locked away behind bars. And the fact that they are locked away does not mean that they need to stay that way. We have forgotten that many Black inmates are simply political prisoners. That is, many are prisoners simply because those who are responsible for their imprisonment have more power than those who are imprisoned. We have forgotten or don't realize that slavery is still legal in this country, constitutionally, if persons are convicted of crimes. Therefore, the Black church needs to show its compassion for the "least of these." Black inmates are a vital part of the Black community. The Black church needs not only to go see about those incarcerated but to hold them in the midst of the community. The same argument can be made for the old, the poor, and so forth; I am reminded that during counseling sessions, the women (whose narratives I shared earlier) recounted how each of them, even when they could not afford it, brought their tithes into the church (as ever reminded to do):

> "Bring the whole tithe into the storehouse, that there
> may be food in my house. Test me in this," says the LORD
> Almighty, "and see if I will not throw open the flood-
> gates of heaven and pour out so much blessing that you
> will not have room enough for it." (Mal. 3:10 [NIV])

Each woman wondered aloud why she had not realized blessings overflowing in her life, even as she tried to live righteously
as well. They each wondered why those who try to do right are
not at least doing better than those who knowingly do wrong:

> And you will again see the distinction between the righ-
> teous and the wicked, between those who serve God
> and those who do not. (Mal. 3:18 [NIV])

These women expressed that they needed to know God's love,
for God's care to be tangible—taking effect on their circumstances—because that was their hope. Yet, even God's church
body of believers seemed not to care enough to even notice their
urgent needs.

But then, the problems of the Black community become completely overwhelming. How can all of the needs be addressed?
Many churches excuse themselves from the immediacy of the
problems by claiming that what is needed is a bigger facility
first. Then, once that is accomplished, it will somehow be easier
to address the magnitude of the problem. The answer is to do
as much as we can right now. Yet the real problem is that we are
so divided in the community that it is hard to get a critical mass
of Black people together to go about accomplishing the task. So
the real answer is: We can do it if we come together. We can do
it if we return to our African roots and remember that what we
need to be about, to be true to God and our "true selves," is
doing whatever we can for the survival and liberation of all of
the people.

That brings me to another element of the community—those
who have different religious beliefs. So what if we Black people
see and worship God differently? If we know about the religious
roots of Christianity, Judaism, Islam, and in most instances
African traditional religions, all have monotheism in common.

The other thing that we have in common is that we are Black people with a common struggle against racial oppression. These two considerations should be enough to unite us. Besides, God can handle the diversity of those who seek to worship the one God:

> Yet a time is coming and has now come when the true worshipers will worship the Father in spirit and truth, for these are the kind of worshipers the Father seeks. God is spirit, and his worshipers must worship in spirit and in truth. (Jn. 4:23–24 [NIV])

The bottom line is that as believers who are Black we need to come together. The Black church is in a position to make advances across religious lines in the name of survival and liberation.

Conclusion

At this point, this book has come full circle. In light of the current situation confronting African Americans, it seems that our present is our past, and our future, if we are not able to go from theory to practice. Clearly, as we live into a new millennium, we know that survival and liberation for African Americans has been the concern for going on four hundred years. In theory, it is possible to envision real potential for change in the years ahead. Yet in practice, so much is at stake in terms of the urgency and tenuousness of relations between institutions, systems, and people who need to come together in a communal approach in order to end the crisis of Black life in America. As an African American woman pastoral theologian who has reflected upon this hard and long, my conviction is that, together, the Black church and those in the field of pastoral theology and care can make great strides in creating a public will for change and can effectively address the pastoral care needs of African Americans in the meantime. Ideally, each institution would practice what it preaches in supporting roles. Ultimately, the Black church would guide the direction of the struggle for survival and liberation, and the field of pastoral theology and care would provide additional pastoral care to augment the pastoral care of the Black church in whatever ways that are needed. Clearly, economic and political support is vital to putting theory into practice. The hope is in the struggle.

Bibliography

Akbar, Na'im. *The Community of Self*. Rev. ed. Tallahassee, Fla.: Mind Productions & Associates, Inc., 1985.

————. *Chains and Images of Psychological Slavery*. Jersey City, N. J.: New Mind Publications, 1983.

————. "The Evolution of Human Psychology for African Americans." In *Black Psychology*, ed. Reginald L. Jones, 3d ed. Berkeley, Calif.: Cobb & Henry, 1991.

————. "Nile Valley Origins of the Science of Mind." In *Nile Valley Civilizations*, ed. Ivan Van Sertima. New Brunswick, N.J.: Journal of African Civilizations, 1985.

Ani, Marimba. *Yurugu: An African-Centered Critique of European Cultural Thought and Behavior*. Trenton, N.J.: Africa World Press, 1994.

Asante, Molefi Kete. *Afrocentricity*. Trenton, N.J.: Africa World Press, 1988.

Baldwin, James. *Price of the Ticket: Collected Nonfiction, 1848–1985*. New York: St. Martin's/Marek, 1985.

Barrett, Leonard E. *Soul Force: African Heritage in Afro-American Religion*. Garden City, N.Y.: Anchor Books, 1974.

Bell, Derrick. *Faces at the Bottom of the Well*. New York: Basic Books, 1992.

Bennett, Lerone, Jr. *Before the Mayflower*. Baltimore: Penguin Books, 1968.

Billingsley, Andrew. *Climbing Jacob's Ladder: The Enduring Legacy of African American Families*. New York: Simon & Schuster, 1992.

Boesak, Allan. *The Finger of God: Sermons on Faith and Responsibility*. Maryknoll, N.Y.: Orbis Books, 1982.

Bowen, Murray. *Family Therapy in Clinical Practice*. New York: Jason Aronson, 1978.

Boyd-Franklin, Nancy. *Black Families in Therapy: A Multisystems Approach.* New York: Guilford Press, 1989.

Bradford, William D. "Money Matters: Lending Discrimination in African American Communities." In *The State of Black America 1993.* Ed. Billy J. Tidwell. New York: National Urban League, 1993.

Brown Douglas, Kelly. *The Black Christ.* Maryknoll, N.Y.: Orbis Books, 1994.

Browning, Don S. *A Fundamental Practical Theology: Descriptive and Strategic Proposals.* Minneapolis: Fortress Press, 1991.

_____. *Religious Thought and the Modern Psychologies: A Critical Conversation in the Theology of Culture.* Philadelphia: Fortress Press, 1987.

_____. "The Influence of Psychology on Theology." In *The New Shape of Pastoral Theology: Essays in Honor of Seward Hiltner.* Ed. William B. Oglesby, Jr. Nashville: Abingdon Press, 1969.

Bruce, Calvin E. "Nurturing the Souls of Black Folk." *Journal of Pastoral Care* 30, no. 4 (December 1976).

Burbridge, Lynn C. "Toward Economic Self-Sufficiency: Independence Without Poverty." In *The State of Black America 1993.* Ed. Billy J. Tidwell. (New York: National Urban League, 1993.

Burck, J. R., and R. J. Hunter. "Pastoral Theology, Protestant." In *Dictionary of Pastoral Care and Counseling.* Ed. Rodney J. Hunter. Nashville: Abingdon Press, 1990.

Burrow, Rufus, Jr. *James H. Cone and Black Liberation Theology.* Jefferson, N.C.: McFarland & Company, 1994.

_____. "The Dignity of the Person and the Urban Poor." *Encounter* 55.3 (Summer 1994).

_____. "Black Males in Prison: The Silence of the Church." *Encounter* 54.1 (Winter 1993).

Butler, Lee, Jr. "Race, Religion, and African American Cultural Identity Formation." Ph.D. diss., Drew University, 1994.

Cannon, Katie G. *Katie's Canon: Womanism and the Soul of the Black Community.* New York: Continuum, 1995.

_____. *Black Womanist Ethics.* Atlanta: Scholars Press, 1988.

Carter, Harold A., Wyatt Tee Walker, and William A. Jones, Jr. *The African American Church: Past, Present, Future.* New York: Martin Luther King Fellows Press, 1991.

Clebsch, William A., and Charles R. Jaekle. *Pastoral Care in Historical Perspective.* Englewood Cliffs, N.J.: Prentice Hall, 1964.

Clinebell, Howard. *Basic Types of Pastoral Care and Counseling.* Nashville: Abingdon Press, 1984.

Coleman, Willie B. "A Study of African American Slave Narratives as a Source for a Contemporary, Constructive Black Theology." Ph.D. diss., Graduate Theological Union, 1993.

_____. "Tribal Talk: Black Theology in Postmodern Configurations." *Theology Today* 50.1 (April 1993).

Comas-Diaz Lillian, and Beverly Greene, eds. *Women of Color: Integrating Ethnic and Gender Identities in Psychotherapy.* New York: Guilford Press, 1994.

Cone, James H., and Gayraud S. Wilmore, eds. *Black Theology: A Documentary History, Volume One, 1966–1979.* 2d and rev. ed. Maryknoll, N. Y.: Orbis Books, 1993.

_____. *Black Theology: A Documentary History, Volume Two, 1980–1992.* Maryknoll, N.Y.: Orbis Books, 1993.

_____. *Cone, James H. Martin and Malcolm and America: A Dream or a Nightmare?* Maryknoll, N.Y.: Orbis Books, 1991.

_____. *A Black Theology of Liberation.* 2d ed. Maryknoll, N.Y.: Orbis Books, 1986.

_____. *Speaking the Truth: Ecumenism, Liberation, and the Black Church.* Grand Rapids, Mich.: Eerdmans, 1986.

_____. *For My People: Black Theology and the Black Church.* Maryknoll, N. Y.: Orbis Books, 1984.

_____. *My Soul Looks Back.* Nashville: Abingdon Press, 1982.

_____. *God of the Oppressed.* San Francisco: Harper & Row, 1975.

_____. *The Spirituals and the Blues: An Interpretation.* New York: Seabury Press, 1972.

_____. *Black Theology and Black Power.* New York: Seabury Press, 1969.

Cooper-Lewter, Nicholas, and Henry H. Mitchell. *Soul Theology: The Heart of American Black Culture.* 2d ed. Nashville: Abingdon Press, 1991.

Couture, Pamela D. *Blessed Are the Poor?: Women's Poverty, Family Policy, and Practical Theology.* Nashville: Abingdon Press, 1991.

_____, and Rodney J. Hunter, eds. *Pastoral Care and Social Conflict.* Nashville: Abingdon Press, 1995.

Daly, Mary. *Beyond God the Father.* Boston: Beacon Press, 1973.

_____. *The Church and the Second Sex.* New York: Harper and Row, 1975.

_____. *Gynecology: The Metaethics of Radical Feminism.* Boston: Beacon Press, 1978.

_____. *Pure Lust: Elemental Feminist Philosophy.* Boston: Beacon Press, 1984.

DeMarinis, Valerie. *Critical Caring: A Feminist Model for Pastoral Psychology.* Louisville: Westminster John Knox Press, 1993.

Du Bois, W. E. B. *The Souls of Black Folks.* New York: Vintage Books, 1990.

_____. *Black Reconstruction in America 1860–1880.* New York: Atheneum, 1970.

Evans, James. *We Have Been Believers: An African American Systematic Theology*. Minneapolis: Fortress Press, 1992.

Fanon, Frantz. *Black Skins, White Masks*. New York: Grove Press, 1967.

_____. *The Wretched of the Earth*. New York: Grove Weidenfeld, 1963.

Fenton, Carroll M., Jr. *The Care of Souls in the Black Church: A Liberation Perspective*. New York: Martin Luther King Fellows Press, 1980.

Franklin, John Hope. *From Slavery to Freedom: A History of Negro Americans*. 3d ed. New York: Alfred A. Knopf, 1967.

Gerkin, Charles V. *The Living Human Document*. Nashville: Abingdon Press, 1984.

Giddings, Paula. *When and Where I Enter: The Impact of Black Women on Race and Sex in America*. New York: Bantam Books, 1984.

Gilkes, Cheryl Townsend. "The Black Church as a Therapeutic Community: Suggested Areas for Research into the Black Religious Experience." *The Journal of the Interdenominational Theological Center* 8.1 (Fall 1980).

Glaz, Maxine, and Jeanne Stevenson Moessner, eds. *Women in Travail and Transition: A New Pastoral Care*. Minneapolis: Fortress Press, 1991.

Graham, Larry K. *Care of Persons, Care of Worlds: A PsychoSystems Approach to Pastoral Care and Counseling*. Nashville: Abingdon Press, 1992.

_____. "From Psyche to System." *Theology Today* 49.3 (October 1992).

Grant, Jacquelyn. *White Women's Christ and Black Women's Jesus*. Atlanta: Scholars Press, 1989.

_____. "Black Theology and the Black Woman." In *Black Theology: A Documentary History, Volume Two, 1980–1992*.

Ed. James H. Cone and Gayraud Wilmore, 2d and rev. ed. Maryknoll, N.Y. Orbis Books, 1993.

_____. "Womanist Theology in North America." *Journal of the Interdenominational Theological Center* 16 (Fall 1988–Spring 1989).

_____. "Prophetic Theology." In *The Karios Covenant.* Ed. Logan Willis. New York: Friendship Press, 1988.

_____. "Womanist Theology: Black Women's Experience As a Source for Doing Theology, With Special Reference to Christology." *Journal of the Interdenominational Theological Center* 13 (Spring 1986).

_____. "Tasks of a Prophetic Church." In *Theology in the Americas: Detroit II Conference Papers.* Eds. Cornel West, Carida Guidote, and Margaret Coakley. Maryknoll, N.Y.: Orbis Books, 1982.

Green, Beverly A. "What Has Gone Before: The Legacy of Racism and Sexism in the Lives of Black Mothers and Daughters." *Women and Therapy* 9.1–2 (1990).

Grier, William H., and Price M. Cobbs. *Black Rage.* New York: Basic Books, 1968.

Hacker, Andrew. *Two Nations: Black and White, Separate, Hostile, Unequal.* New York: Ballantine Books, 1992.

Harding, Vincent. *Hope and History.* Maryknoll, N.Y.: Orbis Books, 1990.

_____. *There is a River: The Black Struggle for Freedom in America.* New York: Vintage Books, 1983.

Harris, Forrest E., Sr., and Donna E. Allen, eds. *A Call to Dialogue and Reflection on: What Does it Mean to Be Black and Christian?* Nashville: Kelly Miller Smith Institute, 1992.

Harris, James H. *Pastoral Theology: A Black Church Perspective.* Minneapolis: Fortress Press, 1991.

_____. "Practicing Liberation in the Black Church." *Christian Century* 107.1 (June 13, 1990).

Hiltner, Seward. *Preface to Pastoral Theology.* New York: Abingdon Press, 1958.

_____. *Theological Dynamics.* Nashville: Abingdon Press, 1972.

Holifield, E. Brooks. *A History of Pastoral Care in America: From Salvation to Self-Realization.* Nashville: Abingdon Press, 1983.

Hollies, Linda H., ed. *Womanistcare: Volume 1.* Evanston, Ill.: Garrett Evangelical Theological Seminary, 1992.

hooks, bell. *Sisters of the Yam: Black Women and Self-Recovery.* Boston: Southend Press, 1993.

_____. *Black Looks: Race and Representation.* Boston: Southend Press, 1992.

_____. *Yearning: Race, Gender, and Cultural Politics.* Boston: Southend Press, 1990.

_____., and Cornel West. *Breaking Bread: Insurgent Black Intellectual Life.* Boston: Southend Press, 1991.

Hopkins, Dwight. *Shoes That Fit Our Feet: Sources for a Constructive Black Theology.* Maryknoll, N. Y.: Orbis Books, 1993.

_____, ed. *Black Theology USA and South Africa: Politics, Culture, Liberation.* Maryknoll, N. Y.: Orbis Books, 1989.

Hopkins, Dwight, and George C. L. Cummings, eds. *Cut Loose Your Stammering Tongue: Black Theology in Slave Narratives.* Maryknoll, N.Y.: Orbis Books, 1991.

Hunter, Rodney J., ed. *Dictionary of Pastoral Care and Counseling.* Nashville: Abingdon Press, 1990.

Hurston, Zora Neale. *Their Eyes Were Watching God.* Reprint. Urbana, Ill.: University of Illinois Press, 1978.

Jenkins, Adlebert H. "A Humanistic Approach to Black Psychology." In *Black Psychology.* Ed. Reginald L. Jones. 3d ed. Berkeley, Calif.: Cobb & Henry, 1991.

Jones, Arthur C. *Wade in the Water: The Wisdom of the Spirituals.* Maryknoll, N.Y.: Orbis Books, 1993.

_____. "Psychological Functioning in African American Adults: Some Elaborations on a Model, with Clinical Applications." In *Black Adult Development and Aging.* Ed. Reginald L. Jones. Berkeley, Calif.: Cobb & Henry, 1989.

Jones, Jacquelyn. *Labor of Love, Labor of Sorrow: Black Women, Work, and the Family, From Slavery to the Present.* New York: Vintage Books, 1985.

Jones, Reginald L., ed. *Black Psychology.* 3d ed. Berkeley, Calif.: Cobb & Henry, 1991.

Kambon, Kobi Kazambe Kalongi (aka Joseph H. Baldwin). *The African Personality in America: An African-Centered Framework.* Tallahassee, Fla.: NUBIAN Nation Publications, 1991.

_____. "Black Psychology and Black Personality: Some Issues For Consideration." *Black Books Bulletin* 4.3 (1976).

_____. "Notes on an Africentric Theory of Black Personality." *The Western Journal of Black Studies* 5.3 (1981).

Lester, Julius. *To Be a Slave.* New York: Scholastic, 1968.

Levine, Lawrence W. *Black Culture and Black Consciousness.* New York: Oxford University Press, 1977.

MacDonald, Coval B. "Methods of Study in Pastoral Theology." In *The Shape of Pastoral Theology: Essays in Honor of Seward Hiltner.* Ed. William B. Oglesby, Jr. New York: Abingdon Press, 1969.

Marable, Manning. *Speaking Truth to Power: Essays on Race, Resistance, and Radicalism.* Boulder, Colo.: Westview Press, 1996.

Miller-McLemore, Bonnie J. "The Human Web: Reflections on the State of Pastoral Theology." *Christian Century* 110.11 (April 7, 1993).

Minuchin, Sal. *Families and Family Therapy.* Cambridge, Mass.: Harvard University Press, 1974.

_____, and C. Fishman, eds. *Family Therapy Techniques.* Cambridge, Mass.: Harvard University Press, 1981.

Mollenkott, Virginia Ramey. *The Divine Feminine: The Biblical Imagery of God as Female.* New York: Crossroads, 1984.

_____. *Speech, Silence, Action! The Cycle of Faith.* Nashville: Abingdon Press, 1980.

_____. *Women, Men, and the Bible.* Nashville: Abingdon Press, 1977.

Morris, Aldon D. *The Origins of the Civil Rights Movement: Black Communities Organizing for Change.* New York: Freedom Press, 1984.

Morrison, Toni. *Beloved.* New York: Alfred A. Knopf, 1987.

_____. *Bluest Eye.* New York: Pocket Books, 1979.

Murray, Charles. *Losing Ground: American Social Policy, 1950–1980.* New York: Basic Books, 1984.

Myers, Linda James. *Understanding an Afrocentric Worldview: Introduction to Optimal Psychology.* Dubuque, Iowa: Kendall/Hunt, 1988.

Neuger, Christie Cozad. "Feminist Pastoral Theology and Pastoral Counseling: A Work in Progress." *Journal of Pastoral Theology* 2 (Summer 1992).

Nobles, Wade W. "African Philosophy: Foundations of Black Psychology." In *Black Psychology.* 3d ed. Ed. Reginald L. Jones. Berkeley, Calif.: Cobb & Henry, 1991.

_____. *African Psychology: Toward Its Reclamation, Reascension, and Revitalization.* Oakland, Calif.: A Black Family Institute, 1986.

_____. *Africanity and the Black Family: The Development of a Theoretical Model.* Oakland, Calif.: A Black Family Institute, 1985.

Oglesby, William B., Jr., ed. *The New Shape of Pastoral Theology.* Nashville and New York: Abingdon Press, 1969.

Papp, P. "Paradoxes." In *Family Therapy Techniques.* Ed. Sal Minuchin and C. Fishman. Cambridge, Mass.: Harvard University Press, 1981.

Paris, Peter J. *The Spirituality of African Peoples: The Search for a Common Moral Discourse.* Minneapolis: Fortress Press, 1995.

Pasteur, Alfred B., and Ivory L. Toldson. *Roots of Soul: The Psychology of Black Expressiveness.* Garden City, N.Y.: Anchor Press/Doubleday, 1982.

Patton, John. *Pastoral Care in Context: An Introduction to Pastoral Care.* Louisville: Westminster John Knox Press, 1993.

_____. *Is Human Forgiveness Possible? A Pastoral Care Perspective.* Nashville: Abingdon Press, 1985.

_____. *Pastoral Counseling: A Ministry of the Church.* Nashville: Abingdon Press, 1983.

Poling, James Newton. *Deliver Us from Evil: Resisting Racial and Gender Oppression.* Minneapolis: Fortress Press, 1996.

Raboteau, Albert. *Slave Religion.* New York: Oxford Press, 1978.

Roberts, J. Deotis. *Black Theology in Dialogue.* Philadelphia: Westminster Press, 1987.

_____. "Black Theology in the Making." In *Black Theology: A Documentary History, Volume One, 1996–1979.* 2d. and rev. ed. Ed. James H. Cone and Gayraud S. Wilmore. Maryknoll, N.Y.: Orbis Books, 1993.

_____. *Roots of a Black Future: Family and Church.* Philadelphia: Westminster Press, 1980.

Ruether, Rosemary Radford. "Crisis in Sex and Race: Black Theology versus Feminist Theology." In *Mission Trends No. 4: Liberation Theologies.* Ed. Gerald Anderson and Thomas Stansky. Grand Rapids, Mich.: Eerdmans, 1979.

_____. "Feminism and Patriarchal Religion: Principles of Ideological Critique of the Bible." In *Journal for the Study of the Old Testament* 22 (February, 1982).

_____. *New Woman, New Earth: Sexist Ideologies and Human Liberation.* New York: Seabury Press, 1975.

_____. *To Change the World: Christology and Cultural Criticism.* New York: Crossroads, 1981.

Russell, Letty. *Becoming Human.* Philadelphia: Westminster Press, 1982.

_____. *The Future of Partnership.* Philadelphia: Westminster Press, 1979.

_____. *Human Liberation in a Feminist Perspective.* Philadelphia: Westminster Press, 1974.

Scanzoni, Letha, and Nancy Hardesty. *All We're Meant to Be: A Biblical Approach to Women's Liberation with Study Guide.* Waco, Tex.: Word Books, 1977.

Scott, Kesho Yvonne. *The Habit of Surviving.* New York: Ballantine Books, 1991.

Silberman, Charles E. *Criminal Violence, Criminal Justice.* New York: Vintage Books, 1978.

Smith, Archie, Jr. *Navigating the Deep River: Spirituality in African American Families.* Cleveland, Ohio: United Church Press, 1997.

_____. *The Relational Self: Ethics and Therapy from a Black Church Perspective.* Nashville: Abingdon Press, 1982.

Smith, Wallace Charles, Jr. *The Church in the Life of the Black Family.* Valley Forge, Pa.: Judson Press, 1985.

Snorton, Teresa E. "The Legacy of the African-American Matriarch: New Perspectives for Pastoral Care." In *Through the Eyes of Women: Insights for Pastoral Care.* Ed. Jeanne Stevenson Moessner. Minneapolis: Fortress Press, 1996.

SteinhoffSmith, Roy. "The Politics of Pastoral Care: An Alternative Politics of Care." In *Pastoral Care and Social Conflict.* Ed. Pamela D. Couture and Rodney J. Hunter. Nashville: Abingdon Press, 1995.

Swinton, David H. "The Economic Status of African Americans During the Reagan-Bush Era: Withered Opportunities, Limited Outcomes, and Uncertain Outlook." In *The State of Black America, 1993*. Ed. Billy J. Tidwell. New York: National Urban League, 1993.

Taylor, Charles. "Black Experience as a Resource for Pastoral Theology." *Journal for Pastoral Theology* 2 (Summer 1992).

Tidwell, Billy J. "African Americans and the 21st Century Labor Market: Improving the Fit." In *The State of Black America, 1993*. Ed. Billy J. Tidwell, New York: National Urban League, 1993.

Townes, Emilie., ed. *A Troubling in My Soul: Womanist Perspectives on Evil and Suffering*. Maryknoll, N.Y.: Orbis Books, 1993.

Walker, Alice. *In Search of Our Mothers' Gardens: Womanist Prose*. San Diego: Harcourt Brace Jovanovich, 1983.

Walker, Theodore, Jr. *Empower the People: Social Ethics for the African American Church*. Maryknoll, N.Y.: Orbis Books, 1991.

West, Cornel. *Race Matters*. Boston: Beacon Press, 1993.

_____. *Prophetic Reflections: Notes on Race and Power*. Monroe, Mass.: Common Courage Press, 1993.

_____. *Prophetic Fragments*. Grand Rapids, Mich.: Eerdmans, 1988.

_____. *Prophecy and Deliverance: An African American Revolutionary Christianity*. Philadelphia: Westminster Press, 1982.

White, Joseph L., and Thomas A. Parham. *The Psychology of Blacks*. 2d ed. Englewood Cliffs, N. J.: Prentice-Hall, 1990.

Wiley, Christine Y. "The Impact of a Parish Based Pastoral Counseling Center on Counselors and Congregation: A Womanist Perspective." D.Min. diss., Garrett-Evangelical Theological Seminary, 1994.

_____. "Ministry of Empowerment: A Holistic Model For

Pastoral Counseling in the African American Community" *Journal of Pastoral Care* 45.4 (Winter 1991).

Williams, Delores S. *Sisters in the Wilderness.* Maryknoll, N.Y.: Orbis Books, 1993.

_____. "Womanist Theology: Black Women's Voices." In *Black Theology: A Documentary History, Volume Two, 1980–1992.* Ed. James H. Cone and Gayraud S. Wilmore. 2d and rev. ed. Maryknoll, N. Y.: Orbis Books, 1993.

Wilmore, Gayraud S., ed. *Black Men in Prison: The Response of the African American Church.* Atlanta: ITC Press, 1990.

_____. "Black Theology and Pastoral Ministry." In *The Pastor as Theologian.* Ed. Earl E. Shelp and Ronald S. Sunderland. New York: Pilgrim Press, 1988.

Wilson, Amos N. *The Falsification of Afrikan Consciousness.* New York: Afrikan World Infosystems, 1993.

_____. *Black-on-Black Violence.* New York: Afrikan World Infosystems, 1990.

Wimberly, Edward P. *Counseling African American Marriages and Families.* Louisville, Ky.: Westminster John Knox Press, 1997.

_____. *Using Scripture in Pastoral Counseling.* Nashville: Abingdon Press, 1994.

_____. "African American Spirituality and Sexuality: Perspectives on Identity, Intimacy, and Power." In *Journal of Pastoral Theology* 4 (Summer 1993).

_____. *African American Pastoral Care.* Nashville: Abingdon Press, 1991.

_____. *Prayer in Pastoral Counseling: Suffering, Healing, Discernment.* Louisville, Ky.: Westminster John Knox Press, 1990.

_____. *Pastoral Counseling and Spiritual Values: A Black Point of View.* Nashville: Abingdon Press, 1982.

_____. *Pastoral Care in the Black Church.* Nashville: Abingdon Press, 1979.

Wimberly, Edward P., and Ann Streaty Wimberly. *Liberation and Human Wholeness: The Conversion Experiences of Black People in Slavery and Freedom.* Nashville: Abingdon Press, 1986.